SKILLS IN
RELIGIOUS
STUDIES

Book  2

FOUNDATION EDITION

S C MERCIER AND J FAGEANT

Heinemann Educational Publishers
Halley Court, Jordan Hill, Oxford, OX2 8EJ
a division of Reed Educational & Professional
Publishing Ltd
Heinemann is a registered trademark of Reed
Educational & Professional Publishing Ltd

OXFORD MELBOURNE AUCKLAND
JOHANNESBURG BLANTYRE GABORONE IBADAN
PORTSMOUTH NH(USA) CHICAGO

© Caroline Mercier and Jo Fageant, 2000
First published 2000

British Library Cataloguing in Publication Data

A catalogue record for this book is available from the
British Library

ISBN 0 435 302086
04 03 02 01 00
10 9 8 7 6 5 4 3 2 1

Designed by Ken Vail Graphic Design, Cambridge
Picture research by Jacqui Rivers
Printed and bound in Great Britain by Bath
Colourbooks, Glasgow

Acknowledgements

The authors and publishers would like to thank the
following for the use of copyright material:
Scriptures quoted from the *Good News Bible* published
by the Bible Societies/HarperCollins Publishers Ltd.,
UK, © American Bible Society, 1966, 1971, 1976, 1992;
The Teaching of Buddha© 1996 by Bukkyo Dendo
Kyokai, Buddhist Promoting Foundation, 3–14, 4-chome,
Shiba, Minato-ku, Tokyo, Japan, 108, 137th revised ed.,
1987 on p. 47; The cover design from *Faith in the City:
The Report of the Archbishop of Canterbury's
Commission on Urban Priority Areas* is copyright© The
Central Board of Finance of the Church of England,
1985; The Archbishops' Council, 1999 and is
reproduced by permission on p.63; Extract from the
Nicene Creed, taken from *The Alternative Service Book
1980* is copyright© The International Consultation on
English texts (ICET) on p.48; The Lord's Prayer in its
modern form is adapted from the International
Consultation on English Texts version on p.61. The
Nicene Creed and Lord's Prayer from *The Alternative
Service Book 1980* are reproduced by permission of the
publishers; Manchester University Press for the
extracts from *Textual sources for the study of Sikhism*
on pp. 85 and 88; The Muslim Educational Trust for
the translated quotations of the Qur'an from *Islam:
Beliefs and Teachings* by Ghulam Sarwar on pp. 64 and
66; Poster produced and published by Ta-Ha
Publishers Ltd. on p. 66; World Council of Churches,
150 Route de Ferney, 1211 Geneva 2, Switzerland for
the badge on p. 55.

The publishers would like to thank the following for
permission to use photographs:
A.K.G. on p. 52; Mark Azavedo on pp. 25, 43, 46, 56,
73, 74; Circa photo library on pp. 6, 7, 8, 11, 22, 23, 26,
28, 31, 34, 41, 44, 48, 55, 59, 68, 70, 78, 92; Garden
Matters on pp. 34, 47; Hutchison Photo Library on pp.
20, 38, 50, 65, 79, 93; Impact Photo Library on pp. 6, 8,
16, 63, 65, 73, 88; Metropolitan Police on p. 5;
Christine Osborne on pp. 28, 39, 40, 53, 59, 61, 83, 86;
Peter Sanders on p. 66, Science Photo Library on p. 4;
Skyscan on p. 49; Travel Ink on p. 46; Trip on pp. 4,
10,12, 13, 14, 20, 21, 29, 30, 35, 36, 37, 44, 45, 50, 54,
57, 64, 67, 69, 71, 73, 75, 76, 77, 79, 80, 82, 84, 85, 86,
87, 90, 91; Tropix Photo Library on p. 76.

The publishers would like to thank Impact/Mohamed
Ansar, James Davis Worldwide, Peter Sanders and
Andes Press Agency/Carlos Reyes-Manzo for
permission to reproduce the cover photographs.

The publishers have made every effort to trace the
copyright holders, but if they have inadvertently
overlooked any, they will be pleased to make the
necessary arrangements at the first opportunity.

Contents

··

··

Faith and authority

How should I live my life?' 'How should I behave towards others?' 'How do I know what is right and what is wrong?' These are some of the difficult questions we have to answer in life. We have some important decisions to make.

Some people say you are on your own. You have to work it out for yourself. Others simply follow the crowd. People who belong to a religious faith say that we are not alone. They believe that there are signposts to help us on our way in life. There are guidelines to follow that others have tried and tested.

B Does the voice of science carry greater authority than the voice of religion today?

Guidelines

Sometimes these guidelines appear as laws or teachings, for example, the Ten Sayings in the Jewish **Torah**. Sometimes the guidance is given through the example of teachers and leaders. Sikhs follow the example of their Ten **Gurus**. Sometimes the guidance comes in stories. For example, the stories Jesus told help Christians to think about how to live their lives.

Sacred writings

Many religious stories and teachings are passed down in the words of sacred scriptures or writings. Believers say that their scriptures contain wisdom and truth. They find comfort and guidance in the teachings. It is this experience that helps to give the scriptures their special authority.

A Do our religious leaders still carry authority?

Religious teachings do not contain easy answers. Sometimes their advice is hard to swallow. They do offer a way that is not based on selfishness, greed, fear or just lack of decision.

C The word of scripture still holds authority for many

Discussion question

What voices of authority do people listen to today? Look at the photos to help you. Can you think of other examples?

Revelation

At the heart of each religion is the belief that the truth has been given to humankind. That is to say the truth is eternal and not a human invention. Many religious people say that it is God who reveals the truth to people. They call their scriptures revelation and believe they carry the authority of God's word.

THINGS TO DO

1 Draw a cartoon or picture to show one of the voices of authority in photos **A**, **B** or **C**. Under your drawing say why people accept the authority you have drawn.

2 People say that some rules are just true – they are 'given' and you have to accept them. For example, 'You shall not kill'. Make a list of six rules that you think are true or 'given'. Compare your ideas with a partner and write out the ones you agree on. Discuss your ideas with the rest of the class.

3 What are the difficult things that people need help with today? Is it the problem of war or poverty, or is it the environment? Write a message in a bottle asking for help with one of the problems of the world. Say what you would like to see in answer to the message.

4 Science is an important authority for many people. What does science say about how the universe came to be or how life on earth began? Science cannot answer questions like: 'Why is there a universe?' or 'How should we live our lives?' Discuss with a partner how you could answer these questions.

New words

Torah   Gurus

Hinduism: Gurus and sacred texts

Hinduism cannot be described in a single set of beliefs and practices. There is no founder.

There are several scriptures, not one. Spiritual truth is revealed through teachers as well as sacred books.

Gurus and spiritual teachers

Many Hindus follow the teachings of a guru or spiritual teacher. For example, Sathya Sai Baba (**A**) has a large following in India and in the UK. His teachings are based on love, truth and peace.

Some Hindus belong to the Krishna Consciousness Movement. They follow the teachings of the Bengali saint, Chaitanya.

He taught his followers to worship **Krishna** as the Supreme Lord God.

Discussion question

In what way is a spiritual teacher different from other teachers?

The scriptures

The Hindu scriptures are used every day in worship at the shrine and in the temple (**B**). Sometimes travelling actors perform the stories. Some of the scriptures are in the ancient Indian language of Sanskrit. Hindus can read them in translation. Children read them in comic-strip books. They can also see the stories on film and video.

There are two main groups of scriptures. One is **Shruti**, which means 'revealed'. Hindus believe that they were revealed to Hindu holy men in ancient India. This

A Sathya Sai Baba has many followers in India and the UK

There is another group of scriptures called **Smriti**, which means 'remembered'. These contain stories such as the Mahabharata and the Ramayana. The best known Smriti text is the **Bhagavad Gita**. It means the 'Song of the Lord'. It contains the words of Lord Krishna.

> **New words**
>
> Krishna   Shruti   Vedas   Upanishads
> atman   Brahman   Smriti
> Bhagavad Gita

THINGS TO DO

1 Make two columns on your page with the headings Shruti and Smriti. Under each heading list the different scriptures and say what they contain.

2 Write three questions you could ask the priest in photo **B** about the sacred book in front of him. For example, you could ask 'When do you read from the book?'. Say how he might answer your questions.

3 If you were only allowed to keep one book for life, which book would you want to keep? Explain your choice. Answer the question in full sentences.

4 Photo **C** is a picture of Gandhi. He was a spiritual teacher and a man of peace as well as a political figure. Is there someone today that you think is a teacher and leader in this way? Design a card or poster showing the person you have chosen and say why you have chosen them.

B Words from the Hindu scriptures are used in worship and in teaching

group of writings contains the **Vedas** and the **Upanishads**. These are the most ancient of the scriptures. The Vedas contain prayers still used in worship today. The Upanishads are teachings about **atman**, the human soul, and **Brahman**, the Supreme Spirit. The word Upanishad means to 'sit down near'. The words were passed on to students who sat down to listen to the holy men teach.

C For some Gandhi is a divine figure and his image is revered

3

What is real?

What lasts forever? What is real? In other words, what can we rely on? A house appears real but it may one day become a heap of bricks. It does not last forever. The ground feels real but one day the earth will come to an end.

All things change. All things pass. Nothing we see or touch, taste or smell will remain forever.

A The Hindu scriptures are looked to for answers to life's questions

Discussion question

Does everything change eventually?

Brahman is real

In the Hindu scriptures (**A**) it says that only one thing is lasting and real. Only Brahman is real. Everything else is **maya**. Maya is the word used for all the things that do not last. Brahman is the Supreme Spirit. Brahman never changes. When everything else is destroyed, Brahman will remain.

There is a story in the Hindu scriptures about a student who wants to know about Brahman. His guru (**B**) tells him to put some salt in a bowl of water. Later there is no sign of the salt. The guru tells him to sip the water from each side of the bowl. From every side the water is salty. Like the salt, Brahman cannot be seen. But we can know that Brahman is everywhere and in everything.

B A guru teaching students and followers

C Samsara – the never-ending cycle of rebirth

Brahman and atman

Hindus believe that Brahman is present in all living creatures. Every creature has a soul. Hindus call this atman. Many Hindus believe that the soul is Brahman. It therefore lives forever. When the body dies the soul lives on. It is born into another body on earth. This cycle of birth, death and rebirth is called **samsara (C)**.

The law of karma

Hindus believe that every action we carry out has an effect. This is the law of **karma**. Karma means actions and the effects of actions. If our actions are good, we are rewarded in the future. If our actions are bad we will suffer or pay for them. Our actions bring us back again and again to live on earth. We are caught in an endless cycle of birth, death and rebirth. The Hindu scriptures tell Hindus how to escape this cycle. This escape or release is called **moksha**. Once the soul is released from the cycle of rebirth it can be united with God (Brahman).

THINGS TO DO

1 Tell the story of the salt in water using words and pictures. Say what the story means.

2 Write three examples of actions that have an effect on the person carrying out the action. For example, someone who is always unkind will not have any friends. Compare your ideas with those of a partner.

3 Draw the diagram of the chain **(C)**. Say how it shows the never-ending cycle of birth, death and rebirth.

4 'Does anything last forever?' Think about the question. Write a poem based on your ideas.

New words

maya   samsara   karma   moksha

Aims for living

The Hindu scriptures describe four aims in life. One is to create wealth or prosperity. This is called **artha**. People want to provide for their family and live in comfort. Some people like to make money and be successful. Hindus believe that this can be a good aim in life if it helps to create wealth for the community. But in the long run it will not bring happiness or peace of mind.

Sense enjoyment

Another aim is physical love and enjoyment. This is called **kama**. Hindus believe that physical love is not to be taken lightly. It is a way of giving and receiving pleasure. It is a gift from God. Hindus believe that wanting a loving sexual relationship within marriage is a good aim in life. But this does not last forever.

A Lord Vishnu is the protector of dharma and religious duty

B Some Hindus give up the comforts of life

Discussion question

How do the aims of artha and kama compare with your aims in life?

Religious duty

Another aim in life is **dharma** (**A**), which means religion or religious duty (see unit 5). A person's duty or dharma depends on their age and position in life. For example, it is the duty or dharma of parents to support and care for their family.

Highest aim

All these aims are important. But the highest goal in life is moksha. Moksha is release from the cycle of endless rebirth, from karma and samsara. The Hindu scriptures say that it is our desires that make us act. Then the soul would be free from samsara.

Yoga and meditation

Some Hindus choose to give up material comforts and desires. They lead a life of an ascetic (**B**). Through **meditation** and **yoga** they control their thoughts and desires. They can then become free from past karma. So at death the soul is released from the cycle of rebirth to find union with God (moksha).

New words

artha   kama   dharma   meditation   yoga

> **THINGS TO DO**

1 Design a poster to illustrate one of the Hindu aims in life.

2 Write down your aims in life. Say how they are the same or different from the Hindu aims in life.

3 The duty or dharma of the student is to work hard at his/her studies. Say what you think that the dharma of a teacher would be according to Hindu teaching.

4 Every action is based on our desires. We may take action to avoid things we hate, or perform action to get something we want. Write down two examples to illustrate this idea. Say how it shows what Hindus believe about action.

5 Duty and righteousness

Dharma means religious duty or law. It means doing what is right. The best-loved teaching on dharma is the story of Rama. Hindus worship Rama as an **avatar** of the god **Vishnu**. An avatar is 'one who comes down'. In other words, God came down to earth as Rama.

Prince Rama

Long ago, in India, there lived a prince called Rama. He was an obedient son and heir to his father's throne. His father, the king, had promised his wife two wishes. She asked that Rama be sent into the forest for fourteen years. She then asked

A Rama and his wife Sita represent the importance of dharma

that her own son be crowned instead. The king kept his promise but died broken-hearted. Rama knew it was his duty to keep his father's promise. So he went into the forest.

In the forest, Rama's wife, Sita, was kidnapped by the demon, Ravana. He threatened the whole world. Rama rescued Sita and destroyed Ravana. After fourteen years Rama returned to be crowned **(A)**. It was his duty as king to keep peace and justice in the land. So Rama put the good of his people before his own comfort. He was true to his dharma.

The four classes

The Hindu scriptures say a person's dharma depends on their place in society. There were four classes in Hindu society. These were called **varnas**. There is a story in the scriptures about a giant. Each part of his body stands for a class. His mouth is the **Brahmin** class, the priests and teachers. His arms are the **Kshatriyas**, the rulers and soldiers. His thighs are the **Vaishyas**, people in business and trade. His feet are the **Shudra** class, the servants and labourers.

Discussion question

What do you think is the duty of:
• parent
• doctor
• teacher
• cleaner?

The scriptures give detailed guidance on the duty or dharma of each class. When each class performs its duty then everyone's needs are met **(C)**.

Other groups grew up within the main classes. These are known as **jati** or castes. Different trades and jobs had different castes. Some jobs were thought to be unclean **(B)**. People in these jobs were

B Those who were once called outcastes now prefer the term dalit or the oppressed – why?

considered outcastes or **untouchables**. In the past these people did not have the same rights as other people. But today it is illegal to treat people in this way. Everyone must be treated fairly.

THINGS TO DO

1 Rama is a model of dharma. He does what is right. Find two occasions in the story when Rama performed his duty or dharma. Write a sentence on each.

2 Draw a picture to show the giant representing the four classes of Hindu society. Label your picture.

3 If everyone did what was right and good do you think fewer people would suffer in society? How can we encourage people to do what is right?

4 Some divisions in a school community are helpful – for example, form classes. Other divisions are not. Write down two examples of divisions which are helpful and two which are not. Explain your answer.

New words

avatar Vishnu varnas Brahmin
Kshatriyas Vaishyas Shudra
jati untouchables

C The dharma of the teacher is to enlighten his or her students

The song of the Lord

One of the best-loved of the Hindu scriptures is the Mahabharata. This is a poem about a war between two royal families. These were the Pandavas, or sons of Pandu, and their cousins, the Kauravas.

King Pandu

There was once a king called Pandu who gave up his throne to go in search of moksha. He asked his brother to act as king and to be like a father to his sons. His brother agreed. But his own sons were jealous of the Pandavas. They robbed them of their land. The Pandavas tried to recover what was theirs. They tried all peaceful means to settle matters. In the end they had to go to battle against their cousins.

A Krishna teaching Arjuna

Arjuna and Krishna

One of the Pandavas called **Arjuna** was a brave warrior. But he was filled with fear and dread when he saw he had to fight his cousins. He asked his charioteer, Krishna (**A**), what he should do. Krishna said it was his duty as a prince and warrior to fight against evil. Even if he had to kill his cousins, their souls would be reborn. Krishna said Arjuna must fight without any hatred or desire for power. In this way he would not get any bad karma. He must fight for what is right and not for himself.

B Those working in this leper rehabilitation centre in India are following the path of unselfish action

Discussion question

Is it possible to act without any selfish desires? Why would it be hard to do this?

Ways to moksha

During the discussion with Arjuna, Krishna shows himself as the Supreme Lord God. This story is called the Bhagavad Gita or the Song of the Lord. In it Krishna goes on to tell Arjuna of three ways to moksha. The first way is **jnana yoga**. This is the way of knowledge. It means giving up possessions and practising yoga and meditation (see page 11). This is a way of burning up past karma that gets in the way of moksha.

The second way to moksha is the way of unselfish action called **karma yoga**. Every action must be dedicated to God. Every action must be done without selfish desires (**B**). In this way no karma builds up.

The third way is the way of loving devotion (**bhakti yoga**). This is explained in Unit 7.

THINGS TO DO

1 Tell the story of the evil Kauravas and the good Pandavas in your own words.

2 Draw Krishna telling Arjuna he must go to battle. Use speech bubbles to include his teaching.

3 Carrying out every action without any personal desire for reward is one way to moksha. Write about one other way.

4 The Hindu way is to do your best but not to desire the results of your actions. Describe three ways to act like this, for example, baking a cake for someone when you know you will not get a piece of it.

New words

Arjuna   jnana yoga   karma yoga
bhakti yoga

7 The way of love

Discussion question

How do people show their love when they are truly in love with someone?

In the Bhagavad Gita, Krishna offers a third way to reach moksha. It is called Bhakti yoga. It means loving God in body, mind and spirit. Every action becomes an act of love for God. Krishna says he will help all who love him. He will bring them release from karma and samsara.

Bhakti yoga

Bhakti yoga encourages the worshipper to see God as a lover and friend. Someone who is in love thinks only about the person they love. They give presents and sing love songs. Hindus show their love for God through offerings and songs.

Loving devotion

Some Hindus recite the many names of God as an act of loving devotion. Followers of the Krishna Consciousness Movement (**A**) chant the names of Rama and Krishna. They believe that in this way they can purify their hearts and fill them with love and devotion to God.

Many Hindus express their love through worship at a **shrine** (**B**). Most Hindus have a shrine in their home. Often the mother gets up as soon as the day begins. She showers and dresses in clean clothes. But she will not put on her shoes. She

A Members of the Krishna Consciousness Movement sing their love for Krishna

B Hindus worship in the home with offerings of food

approaches the shrine and bows before the **deity**. She rings a bell. She then washes the image of the deity. Offerings of **incense**, flowers and food are placed before the image. Then a **ghee lamp** is lit and held up before the image. The mother may recite hymns and prayers.

In the evening the family may worship at the shrine. They will make offerings of food. This then becomes blessed food which will be added to the evening meal.

Meditation

Many Hindus meditate each day. Some use yoga exercises to help them control and calm the body and mind. They may sing **bhajans** (hymns) and repeat **mantras** (prayers).

New words

shrine   deity   incense   ghee lamp
bhajans   mantras

THINGS TO DO

1 Design a poster to show the way of bhakti yoga. Show how it is one of the three ways to moksha in Hinduism. Look back to unit 6 to help you.

2 'The way of Bhakti is like being in love with God.' Copy out this statement. Now find evidence from these two pages to show that this is true.

3 What would you expect to find in a Hindu home that you would not find in a non-Hindu home? Write your answer as a conversation between a Hindu and a non-Hindu.

4 How can you tell from the photos that worship is about inner feelings as well as outward actions?

8 The temple

The Hindu temple is called a **mandir**. In India, a mandir is the house of a god or goddess. A priest takes care of the image of the deity. Worshippers go to the temple just as they might visit a close friend. They stop to pray or to make an offering. The temple can be very elaborate like the one in the photo (**A**). Or it can be very simple.

The mandir in the UK

In the UK, the mandir may be in a converted hall or church. There is usually a large shrine room where people meet for worship. There are often many shrines (**B**). Each contains an image of a different god or goddess. The images are called **murtis**.

Regular services

In the UK, Hindus often gather for the **arti** service once a week. Worshippers take off their shoes when they enter the temple. They bow down before the deities and make offerings of food or money. Later this is shared in the community. Everyone sits on the floor for worship. They may sing songs of praise while the priest prepares the murtis (images). These are washed and dressed. Offerings of food and flowers are placed before them. When the priest is ready, everyone stands for the offering of light.

A In India, a mandir is the house of a deity

B In the UK the mandir may have many shrines

Community centre

Worshippers may visit the temple even when there is no service. They make offerings at the shrine. This is called **puja**. They also pray, meditate or listen to readings from the scriptures. The temple is often a community centre. For example, there may be coffee mornings or mother and toddlers groups. Many temples run a youth club. Most young Hindus were born in the UK. However, they may speak Gujurati or Punjabi at home. The temple may offer language classes so that they can learn to read and write in their mother tongue.

Discussion question

Why do you think that Hindus in the UK like to get together for worship?

To Hindus, loving God is shown in love for other people. So friendship and service to others are important. Volunteers help to run the temple and raise money for charities.

THINGS TO DO

1 Divide a page into two columns. On one side write three sentences about the mandir in India. On the other side write three sentences about the mandir in the UK.

2 Design a Hindu temple showing the shrine room.

3 Write a timetable for a week in a mandir in the UK. Include times for worship as well as community events.

4 Loving God should be shown through love towards others. Write three sentences giving examples of how Hindus might show love for God in this way.

New words

mandir   murtis   arti   puja

---

9 Who are the Jews?

Jews can be Jews by being born to a Jewish mother. They can also be people who follow the religion of Judaism.

The Jewish race

Tradition says that the Jewish people came from the family of the **prophet Abraham** and his grandson **Jacob**. Jacob became known as **Israel**. The land where Jewish people settled also became known as Israel. Wars forced many to leave.

Over the years Jewish communities developed all over the world (**A**, **B** and **C**). In some countries they lived separately. Often they were not given the same rights as other people.

Discussion question

Sometimes groups are forced to live separately. Why do you think groups in school, or in society, choose to keep themselves separate?

A These young Jews in Jerusalem came from Ethiopia

B A Jew in a synagogue in Kerala, India

Judaism throughout the world

Jewish people made a difference in countries where they lived. Other people were influenced by them. In turn, Jewish traditions were influenced by the societies in which they lived.

In most countries Jews now have the same rights as everyone else. They live and work alongside non-Jewish neighbours. They are Jewish, but they also think of themselves as British, French or American, for example.

So who is Jewish?

Marriage between Jews and non-Jews often takes place. Sometimes the non-Jewish partner chooses to become a Jew. Children born in families like these will probably be brought up as practising religious Jews.

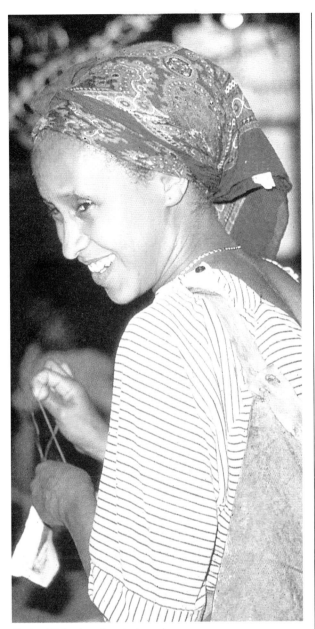

C An Ethiopian Jew in Israel

Some Jews choose not to keep the traditions and practices of Judaism. This does not mean they stop being Jewish.

Most Jews are born into Jewish families but it is possible to choose to become a Jew by following the Jewish religion.

Jews live in many countries of the world. The largest groups are in the United States of America and Israel.

New words

prophet   Abraham   Jacob   Israel

THINGS TO DO

1 It is a good idea for people who want to get married to have some things in common. They might share hobbies, beliefs and values. They might come from the same backgrounds. What difficulties might arise if two people from different religious backgrounds marry?

2 In most countries where Jews live they now have the rights of full citizens. This has not always been true. Britain has laws which try to make sure that everyone is treated equally. How can laws help to give everyone equal rights? What else might be needed to make sure people do not suffer from prejudice and discrimination?

3 Many Jews see Israel as their spiritual home. Some strict Jews would like the religious practices of Judaism to be a strong influence in the way the country is run. Many non-religious Jews do not want the country to be strongly influenced by religion. What difficulties might these different views cause?

4 At some times in history Jews have been forced to leave their homes and live elsewhere. People in many areas of the world today are forced into similar situations. Many have to become refugees. What are some of the difficulties and sadnesses they might face? How might a religious faith help in such situations?

10 The Tenakh

Jewish scriptures are known as the **Tenakh**. The word Tenakh is made from the first letters of three other words: Torah, Nevi'im and Ketuvim. These are the names of the three sections of the Jewish Bible.

Ketuvim

Ketuvim means 'writings'. This section contains several different sorts of books. For example, Ruth and Esther are read on festival occasions (**A**). Others, like Psalms, Proverbs and Ecclesiastes provide thoughts about God and his teachings. They also show people how they should live life.

> 'The Lord is merciful and good; our God is compassionate. The Lord protects the helpless.'

Discussion question

What impression of God is created by these verses from Psalm 116?

Nevi'im

Nevi'im means 'prophets'. A prophet was believed to be a messenger of God. The prophets of Israel reminded other Jews of how God wanted them to live.

Torah

The most important part of the Tenakh is the **Torah**. Torah means 'teaching'. It contains the five books of Moses. Tradition says God gave Moses both the written and the oral, or spoken, Torah. The written Torah contains God's instructions for living. The oral Torah explains these laws so people understand them more fully. When the oral Torah was eventually written down it was called the **Mishnah**.

A The story of Esther is read during the festival of Purim

The Talmud

Rabbis, or teachers, have studied the Torah and Mishnah. Their thoughts and ideas have been written down in the **Gemara**. The Mishnah and Gemara help to explain the Torah. Together they are called the **Talmud**. This helps Jews understand what God's instructions mean in their lives today.

Understanding the scriptures

Orthodox Judaism teaches that the Torah is the word of God exactly as it was revealed to Moses. The instructions are followed even today because they are still important.

Reform Judaism teaches that the Torah was written by people who were inspired by God. They were also influenced by the ideas of their times.This means some of the instructions they wrote need not be followed today

B Students still debate the Torah and Talmud

THINGS TO DO

1 Choose one of the following verses from the Book of Proverbs and make a poster to show its meaning:

'It is better to have a little, honestly earned, than to have a large income gained dishonestly.'

(Proverbs 16:8)

'Kind words bring life, but cruel words crush your spirit.'

(Proverbs 15:4)

2 Prophets sometimes criticized what people did and said. Both giving and receiving criticism can be difficult. Discuss with a partner the reasons why this is so.

3 Rabbis still study and debate the details of the Torah and Talmud (**B**).It has been traditional for this to be done in pairs. What do you think might be the advantages of this?

4 The Talmud is important for understanding the meaning of the Torah. It is the work of very clever rabbis. In groups discuss what you think is meant by the following quotation. What meaning does it have today?

'Respect your father and your mother.'

(Exodus 20:12)

What does it mean to respect your parents? How can young people show respect? What relevance has this to children who do not live with their parents?

New words

Tenakh Ketuvim Nevi'im Torah
Mishnah Rabbis Gemara Talmud
Orthodox Judaism Reform Judaism

The synagogue

When the Jewish people had a settled life in Israel, the temple in Jerusalem was the centre of worship. In the sixth century BCE many people were forced to leave Israel and to live elsewhere. They tried to meet in groups to hear the scriptures and worship together. Places where they met became known as **synagogues**, or 'meeting places'. The synagogue is the place where Jews meet, study and pray.

Inside a synagogue

In synagogues the scrolls of the Torah are kept in a cupboard. The cupboard is in the wall facing Jerusalem. It is called the **Ark.**

Discussion question

Why do you think the Ark is found in the wall which faces Jerusalem?

Above the Ark there is often a quotation. Sometimes 'Know before whom you stand' is written in Hebrew. This reminds Jews that God is everywhere. There is often a model of the two stone tablets on which Moses received the **Ten Sayings** or Ten Commandments.

There are often two prayers on either side of the Ark. One is for the state of Israel and the other is for the country the synagogue is in. In Britain this would be a prayer in English for the Royal Family. The prophet Jeremiah told people that God said:

'Work for the good of the cities where I

A Inside an Orthodox synagogue

B Inside a Reform synagogue

have made you go…Pray to me on their behalf.'

(Jeremiah 29:7)

In front of the Ark there is a small lamp called the **Ner Tamid**. It is kept alight as a reminder of the lamp which was always burning in the temple in Jerusalem.

The reading of the Torah

The reading of the Torah is an important part of synagogue services. This takes place on a platform called the **bimah**.

Organization of a synagogue

In Orthodox synagogues men and women sit separately. Women might be in a gallery, which sometimes has a screen. Services are led by men. In Reform synagogues men and women sit together and services may be led by men or women.

New words

synagogue	Ark	Ten Sayings
Ner Tamid	bimah	

THINGS TO DO

1 Photo **A** is of an Orthodox synagogue and photo **B** is of a Reform synagogue. What clues show you which is which?

2 Some say the Ner Tamid is a symbol that the light of the Torah will shine forever. Psalm 119:5 expresses a similar idea:

'Your word is a lamp to guide me and a light for my path.'

Create a symbol to show what this means.

3 The prophet Jeremiah said people should work for the community in which they live. Discuss ways you could work for the good of:
   • your school
   • your local community.

4 Suggest some benefits of men and women:
   • worshipping separately
   • worshipping together.

The Torah

The work of a scribe

The five Books of Moses (see page 22) are written in Hebrew on a scroll called the **Sefer Torah**. It is handled with the greatest care. The words are handwritten by a scribe. They are written on parchment made from the skins of **kosher** animals.

The work of a scribe is very skilled (**A**). There must be no mistakes in the Sefer Torah. If he makes a mistake, the ink has to be removed form the parchment with a knife. It takes at least a year to write a whole scroll.

B Torah scrolls in an open Ark

A A scribe writing a Torah scroll

Dressing the Sefer Torah

The Sefer Torah is rolled on two wooden poles with handles. Often the scroll is wrapped in an embroidered cover. Over this hangs a silver breastplate and a **yad**. This is a pointer in the shape of a hand with a pointing finger. It is used to help the reader follow the words. A silver crown, often with bells, is placed over the top of the two poles. Sometimes a crown is placed on each pole (**B**).

Some Jews dress the Torah in this way. Others put the scrolls in decorated wooden or metal cylinders (**C**).

C A Sefer Torah dressed in the Sephardim tradition

Discussion question

Why do you think Jews choose to dress the Sefer Torah in these special ways?

The Torah in the synagogue

Passages from the Torah are read in synagogue services. Someone from the congregation opens the Ark. The scroll is taken out and carried to the bimah. As it passes by, people lean forward to touch the cover with the tassels of their **tallitot**. Then they kiss the tassels.

A section of the Torah is read each week. This means the whole scroll can be read in a year. It is read during services on Saturday, Monday and Thursday mornings. On a day called **Simchat Torah**, the last section is read. Straight afterwards the first section is read. The cycle of reading then begins again.

Simchat Torah means rejoicing over the Torah. It is a great honour to be chosen to read the Torah on this day.

New words

Sefer Torah   kosher   yad   tallitot
Simchat Torah

THINGS TO DO

1 Although Torah scrolls are very expensive, a synagogue needs to have more than one. Explain in your own words why this is so.

2 Write and illustrate a leaflet which explains why the Torah is important for Jews and how they show this.

3 The Torah is read in Hebrew. What do you think are the advantages and difficulties of this for Jews all over the world?

4 Imagine you are going to interview a Jewish person about Simchat Torah. What questions would you ask and why?

13 Prayer and worship

Jews can say their daily prayers anywhere. However, some synagogues hold daily services because it is important for people to pray together. The most popular services are on Friday evening and Saturday morning because this is Shabbat.

Before worship can take place in Orthodox synagogues, there must be ten male Jews over the age of thirteen there. This is called a **minyan**. In the Reform tradition the ten can be men or women.

Reading the Torah

The Sefer Torah is read in some services. It is taken out of the Ark and a special blessing is said. The scroll is carried to the bimah (**A**). There it is opened and read in Hebrew (**B**).

B A scroll being read at the bimah

Each week ordinary people are called to the bimah for the reading. Many find it hard to read the Hebrew. It is without vowels and the tune for each section has

A The Sefer Torah in a synagogue

to be known by heart. So that no one is embarrassed, someone reads for those who cannot. Each person called to the bimah says the blessings at the beginning and end of their section though.

Prayers

The **Shema** is said during morning and evening services. It states the Jewish belief that there is only one God. Prayers from the Talmud are recited. Prayers are also said for Israel and the country the synagogue is in. A prayer called the **Aleinu** comes at the end of the service. It is about the greatness of God and his covenant (agreement) with the Jewish people.

Synagogue services

Services are not always led by rabbis. The **chazan** who can chant the notes correctly leads the prayers. There are prayer books in Hebrew with a translation for those who cannot read it (**C**). Many Reform synagogues have parts of the service in the language of the country they are in. The atmosphere at the synagogue is friendly and relaxed. There is usually a hall and kitchen where people can meet socially after the service.

C A Hebrew prayer book with an English translation

New words

Shabbat   minyan   Shema   Aleinu chazan

Discussion question

What do you think are the benefits of having a social gathering after a religious service?

THINGS TO DO

1 Some Jewish men dress in special ways for prayer. When we go out or meet someone important we may dress up. What does it show when we do this? What do you think it means when religious people wear special clothes for worship?

2 The Talmud suggests you should say 100 blessings a day. How many things do you feel grateful for in a day? Make a list of them.

3 It is kind to get someone to read from the Torah for those who find it difficult. It is also a way of making sure that the Torah is always read and heard correctly. Why is this important?

4 For Jews the Torah is a symbol of God's love and help. Design a symbol to represent God's love and help. Explain what your symbol means.

Shabbat in the home

Jews meet in synagogues to worship and study together. However, some people say the home is the centre of Jewish life. It is here that Judaism is taught and lived.

Preparation for Shabbat

Jewish life revolves around Shabbat. Jews believe God told them to keep the seventh day of the week holy. Shabbat is a day which is different from other days. In many homes it is a day for the family to be together. Everything has to be got ready. This is because no work is done for 24 hours.

Just before the sun sets on Friday evening the mother of the household lights two candles to welcome the day (**A**). She says a blessing.

Some people may go to the synagogue service before going home for a special Friday night meal.

Discussion question

Jewish tradition says each day begins in the evening. This suggests that sleep is a preparation for the day. What do you think of this idea?

A A Shabbat table

The Friday night meal

Before the meal the father blesses his children and praises his wife. Then he recites or sings **Kiddush**. This is the blessing over the wine. Even the children drink some.

The **challot** are then blessed. These are two loaves of special bread for Shabbat. Everyone has a piece of the first slice which is sprinkled with a little salt. This is a reminder of the salt sprinkled on sacrifices which used to be made in the Temple. Shabbat is a time to think about God and his teachings.

B Havdalah is said at the end of Shabbat

Havdalah

Shabbat ends when three faint stars can be seen in the sky on Saturday evening. At the close of Shabbat a prayer called **Havdalah** is said (**B**). The Havdalah separates Shabbat from the new week. When the Havdalah is said a long plaited or twisted candle is lit. At the same time a little box of sweet spices is lifted up and passed around the family for everyone to smell the last sweetness of Shabbat.

At the end of Shabbat the father takes a sip of sweet wine.

New words

Kiddush   challot   Havdalah

THINGS TO DO

1 In what ways is Judaism learned by living it?

2 Write an article or create a poster to describe and explain how Jews celebrate Shabbat. Use this unit and unit 13.

3 What do you think might be some of the benefits and challenges of having a family day each week?

4 Jews believe God told them not to work on Shabbat. They were told there were 39 activities that they must not do. For example, they must not sew or build and light fires. Rabbis explain how this applies to modern life. What do you think it means to not work on Shabbat? How would putting this idea into practice change:

- what you do?

- what members of your family do?

15

Learning and living Judaism

Education

Education is an important part of Jewish life. Many synagogues provide classes on Sundays, and sometimes in evenings so young people can learn more about their religion. They are encouraged to study the scriptures and learn to read Hebrew (**A**).

Members of the Jewish community train to teach in these 'religion schools'. In some, classes are only for young people up to the age of thirteen. Others also teach older children. Some offer GCSE courses in religious studies and/or Hebrew.

Discussion question

What would you be prepared to spend time studying outside school hours?

Some parents send their children to Jewish schools if there is one in nearby (**B**). Here lessons in Hebrew and Judaism are built into the timetable.

A Children studying Hebrew

B A Jewish day school in London

Following a Jewish way of life

Jews believe God will judge them by how well they have followed his teachings. This is not just about knowing and keeping all the mitzvot or commandments. Many Jews believe they have to want to do what God asks.

To some, for example Orthodox Jews, this will mean strictly keeping all the laws and applying them to modern life.

For all Jews it will mean trying to develop the personal qualities which help them to show God's love for the whole world. This idea is shown in Leviticus 19:17-18:

> 'Do not bear a grudge against anyone, but settle your differences with him…Do not take revenge on anyone or continue to hate him, but love your neighbour as you love yourself.'

Jews believe God wants them to be truthful, honest and fair. Courtesy and good manners are encouraged. The Book of Proverbs says:

> 'A gentle answer quietens anger, but a harsh one stirs it up.'
>
> (15:1)

Many Jews believe God will judge them on their intentions, not on how correctly they have followed his instructions. For example, there are many different reasons for giving gifts. A famous Jewish teacher called Moses Miamonides said there were different kinds of givers. These include those who give when they are asked, those who give without being asked, and those who give without anyone knowing.

Jews believe that those who give generously without thinking of what they can get back live in the way God wants them to.

THINGS TO DO

1 Many people would agree that it is good to be truthful, honest and fair. Why is it sometimes difficult to live up to this? Give examples.

2 Giving gentle answers in angry situations needs great patience. Write a story to show how patience can help in difficult times.

3 Think about why education and learning are important for Jews. What have you valued most in your education so far? Discuss your thoughts in class.

4 What kind of personal qualities would you like to develop? Explain why.

16 The Buddha's enlightenment

B uddhism started in India. It spread through many countries and grew in many ways.

All forms of Buddhism have grown from the teachings of one man called Gotama Buddha. The word **Buddha** means 'Enlightened Being'. Buddhists believe there have been and will be other Buddhas.

Enlightenment

When Gotama gained **enlightenment** it was as if he had woken from a dream. He could understand the truth about life for the first time. He was filled with compassion for people who were struggling through the difficulties of life. He decided to devote the rest of his life to helping others and teaching them the way to **Nibbana** (A).

A A Buddha **rupa** showing the Buddha teaching

Discussion question

Think of times when you have come to understand something clearly for the first time. How did this make you feel?

The Four Noble Truths

The Buddha's teachings about life became known as the **Four Noble Truths**.

- He explained that everyone has times of unhappiness and suffering.

- He said he had discovered the reasons why life is like this. People always seem to want more or something different. When they have what they want, they worry about losing it. People are often filled with a sense of their own importance. They want to have things which they think will make them happy. The Buddha said this was not possible because everything changes. Nothing lasts forever. The Buddha knew that people find it hard to accept that their own lives will not go on forever.

- The way to stop unhappiness and

B A lotus flower in bloom

suffering is to stop wanting.

- The way to stop wanting is to follow the **Eightfold Path** (see unit 17).

New words

Buddha   enlightenment   Nibbana
Four Noble Truths   Eightfold Path
rupa

THINGS TO DO

1 The lotus plant (**B**) is often used as a symbol of enlightenment. It grows in deep muddy water and becomes a beautiful flower. By following the right path people can move away from unhappiness and suffering and gain enlightenment. Enlightenment is also said to be like waking from a dream. What other descriptions or symbols could you use?

2 The Buddha said wanting things makes people unhappy. They cannot keep things forever because everything changes. He encouraged his followers to think for themselves. He suggested they should test out what he said. Do you agree with his description of life? Explain your reasons.

3 According to the Buddha, discontent and unhappiness is caused by wanting. Do you agree? Think of three examples of discontent or unhappiness. In pairs, discuss the causes behind each example.

4 The Buddha said people's greed, hatred and ignorance caused them to want. Look at the Buddhist wheel of eternal rebirth (**C**). The cockerel is a symbol of greed, the snake for hatred and the pig for ignorance. Discuss why each of these was chosen. Make up your own symbols for greed, hatred and ignorance.

C The Buddhist wheel of eternal rebirth

The Dhamma

The middle way

The Buddha's teachings are called the **Dhamma**. He gave his followers advice on how to find peace. These guidelines are called the Eightfold Path. It sets out a middle way. The Buddha said people should not live life in luxury because this distracts them from the spiritual path. Nor should they live in great hardship because people who do can only concentrate on surviving.

The Eightfold Path

The eight parts to this path are not steps to be followed one after another. They all work together to help people towards Nibbana.

- Right understanding   This means waking up to the truth about the way things are. The Buddha said people need to understand that everything changes. People like the security of things and people they know. Relationships change and people die. This belief that nothing lasts is called **anicca**. The Buddha said when we want things to stay the same we only make ourselves and others unhappy.

- Right thought   Thoughts of greed, hatred and envy or jealousy make a person feel unhappy with their life as it is.

- Right speech   This means trying to be truthful and helpful in what you say. Avoid gossip.

- Right action   People should try to be kind to all living beings. For many Buddhists this means they will not eat meat.

A A flower in bud

B A flower in full blossom

C The blossom withers and dies

- Right livelihood   The Buddha said people should earn their living honestly without harming others.

- Right effort   People must work to overcome greed, hatred and ignorance.

- Right mindfulness or awareness This means being very clear about your intentions in life. It also means accepting that everything changes.

DISCUSSION QUESTION

How might Buddhist teachings help you deal with change that you don't want?

- Right concentration   This happens through meditation (see unit 22) and self-discipline.

The Buddha told his followers to teach the Dhamma and be kind and considerate.

New words

Dhamma   anicca   meditation

THINGS TO DO

1 The photos (**A**, **B** and **C**) in this unit show how a flower changes and dies. Design your own symbol of change.

2 Think about some parts of the Eightfold Path and their opposites. Copy out the headings below in your book. Fill in examples under each heading.

- Right speech
- Right action
- Right livelihood
- Wrong speech
- Wrong action
- Wrong livelihood

3 Why might a person living a life of great luxury or great hardship find it difficult to concentrate on spiritual things?

4 The Buddha taught that a person's intentions are very important. Discuss examples of how bad things can happen even when people have good intentions. Also how good things can happen even when people have bad intentions. Do you think intentions are important? Explain your answer.

The Sangha

The Buddha's first **disciples** gave up their usual lives to become wandering monks. They meditated and taught the Dhamma. Some Buddhists today still choose to join communities of **monks** and **nuns**.

'Those who receive alms'

Monks and nuns of the **Theravada** tradition are known as bhikkhus and bhikkhunis. This means 'those who receive **alms**'. They depend on the local community for gifts of food. The community of monks and nuns is called the **Sangha**. In some places this word is used to mean all members of the Buddhist community.

Daily life

Theravada monks and nuns who live in Buddhist countries go into the local area after breakfast with their alms bowls to collect food for the day (**A**). **Lay** Buddhists think it is a privilege to support them.

Western Buddhist groups do not rely on gifts from lay Buddhists. They may run businesses so the Sangha can be self-supporting.

Each day monks and nuns meditate (**B**). They remember the Buddha. They study the Dhamma. Many say, 'I take refuge in the Buddha, I take refuge in the Dhamma and I take refuge in the Sangha.' These are called the **Three Jewels**.

Buddhist Precepts

All Buddhists try to keep Five Precepts. They should:

A Buddhist monks receiving alms in Bangkok, Thailand

B Buddhist nuns meditating

1 Not kill or injure living creatures

2 Not take what is not given

3 Not misbehave sexually

4 Not lie or speak wrongly

5 Not drink alcohol or misuse drugs

When they enter the Sangha, monks and nuns keep five more precepts. They should also:

6 Not eat after midday

7 Not take part in entertainments such as music and dancing

8 Not use jewellery and perfumes

9 Not sleep in a luxury bed

10 Not handle money.

Discussion question

What do you think you would miss most if you lived as a Buddhist monk? What might you gain by living like this?

Theravada monks and nuns only own a bowl, their robes and a razor. They shave their heads as a sign of living simply and giving up self-pride.

New words

disciples   monks   nuns   Theravada
alms   Sangha   lay   Three Jewels

THINGS TO DO

1 Buddhist monks and nuns have very few possessions. Write a short article about the things they have and what they mean.

2 A refuge is a place of safety or protection. Design a poster to show what things people normally take refuge in, in our society.

3 The Five Precepts are advice on what people should not do. Write a positive version of each precept. In other words, what should people aim for?

4 Theravada monks and nuns are noticeable in Britain because they wear robes and shave their heads. Members of western Buddhist groups choose not to stand out in this way. They often do not wear robes or shave their heads. Discuss what you think are the advantages of both approaches to Buddhism in Britain.

Buddhist scriptures

The word 'Dhamma' can be translated in many ways. It can mean 'the truth about the way things are'. It can also mean 'law' or 'what is right'. It can also be 'teaching' or the 'Word of the Buddha'.

The Buddha said no one should just accept his teaching. Each person must test it for themselves in their own life.

Written scriptures

The Buddha's first followers memorized his teachings. The words were handed down in many languages. The most complete collection of these teachings is in **Pali**. The scriptures of the Theravada tradition are called the **Pali Canon**. They are also called the **Tipitaka** or the three baskets. This contains the sayings of the Buddha, his rules for bhikkhus, and discussions about his teachings.

Mahayana Buddhists have other scriptures as well. All these teachings help people on the path to enlightenment.

Many Buddhist Sangha have a library with copies of the scriptures so that people can study them (**A**). Sometimes the scriptures are displayed in the shrine or meditation room. Some copies have been hand-written on palm leaves (**B**).

Different ways of learning

The Buddha knew that people needed to

A Buddhist monks studying the scriptures

B Buddhist scriptures written on palm leaves

be taught in a variety of ways to help them to understand as fully as possible. He was quite happy for the Dhamma to be translated. Sometimes he used stories to help people remember and understand his teachings.

New words

Pali   Pali Canon   Tipitaka
Mahayana

Discussion question

Stories have been used by many great teachers. Why do you think this is so?

The story of Kisa Gotami shows how people can learn from experiences.

Kisa Gotami was the mother of a young boy. Her son became ill and died. She was very upset and she asked people for medicine. Of course, no one could help her. A wise man suggested she should ask the Buddha for help. The Buddha sent her to collect three grains of mustard seed. Each one had to come from a house in which no one had ever died. As Kisa Gotami went from home to home she found that every household had lost a loved one. Everyone had a sadness in their life. Humbled by what she had learnt, she cremated her son and returned to be a follower of the Buddha.

THINGS TO DO

1 Imagine Buddhist scriptures written on palm leaves are going to be part of a local book exhibition. Each book needs an information card by it. Write the card to go with the Buddhist scriptures.

2 Read the story about Kisa Gotami. She learnt from her experience. Write about an experience which taught you or someone else a lesson.

3 For years the Buddha's teachings were taught from memory by teachers. Later they were written down. What do you think are the advantages of learning by:

• listening to a teacher

• reading written ideas and information?

4 The Buddha encouraged people to test out his teachings in their own lives. He wanted people to think for themselves. How important is it for people to think for themselves? Do you think it is easy? Explain your answers.

Supporting one another

Rebirth

The Buddha said that there is no such thing as the 'self' which stays unchanged. However, Buddhists believe in **rebirth**. They say people are made up of feelings, thoughts and beliefs which change all the time. These will carry on in a new life but will be combined in different ways.

Kamma

What the next life will be like depends on what people have chosen to do in this one. Actions that affect life are called a person's **kamma**. This is a sort of unwritten record of what a person has done. Good kamma leads to improvements in this life and the next. Bad kamma makes things worse. The Buddha said a person's kamma depends on what they intended to do. Things that happen by accident do not count.

Giving and receiving

The Buddha taught that people should show loving kindness (**metta**) to all living beings. This idea is shown in the ways **monastic** (monks and nuns) and lay communities help one another. In the Theravada tradition, lay Buddhists provide food and money for monks and nuns.

They believe this earns them **merit** (spiritual reward). The monks and nuns provide teaching and spiritual guidance to help others towards Nibbana.

This relationship is an important part of Buddhism even in countries, like Britain, where there are not many Buddhists. Instead of the monks and nuns going out to receive food, Buddhists can visit monasteries to take food for the Sangha. The food is often received in silence (**A**).

Before eating, the Sangha recites a traditional blessing. Those who brought the food listen quietly and thoughtfully.

Discussion question

Why do followers of many religions say blessings or give thanks for food before they eat it? Can others learn anything from this practice?

A Monks and nuns receiving food in a temple

B People listening to a Buddhist teacher in a London temple

Learning from the Sangha

Visitors are welcome at Buddhist centres belonging to all the major branches of Buddhism (Theravada, Mahayana and **Vajrayana**). People go to learn about Buddhism and ask advice from the Sangha (**B**). Lessons are also given in meditation (see unit 22). Some communities also offer classes for children.

The Sangha shows how people can live happily without wealth and possessions.

New words

rebirth   kamma   metta   monastic
merit   Vajrayana

THINGS TO DO

1 The Buddha said that everything we do has effects somewhere else. Do you agree? Is there anything you do which does not affect anyone or anything else? How much of your life is affected by what others do?

2 Explain ways in which the lay and monastic communities support one another in Buddhism.

3 The Buddha said things we do and say leave an impression on other people even after we have gone. When you leave school, how would you like your teachers and fellow students to remember you? Do you think this is the impression you have created so far? Explain your answers.

4 When the first Buddhist communities were set up in Britain some people did not like them. Others were welcoming. Imagine a Buddhist Sangha is to be set up in your area. Write a letter to the local newspaper about the hopes and concerns of people in the area. Or write about the hopes of the Buddhist community.

The shrine

Many Buddhists have a Buddha rupa, or image, on a high shelf in their homes. It reminds them of the Buddha and his teaching. Offerings of **incense**, light and flowers are often put in front of it.

Discussion question

Why do you think the Buddha rupa is usually placed on a high shelf?

Body, speech and mind

Buddhists often meditate alone. Many choose to join with others at shrines as well. Shrines are always beautiful. Many contain a Buddha rupa. As people enter they often put their hands together to bow to it. They might stand in front of it and with their hands together touch their forehead, mouth and chest. This is a sign that the body, speech and mind are all involved in offering devotion. People sit quietly looking at the image or meditating.

A Mahayana shrines might have images of buddhas and bodhisattvas other than Gotama Buddha

B Prayer wheels are common in Tibet

Mantras

Some people find it helpful to repeat the words of a **mantra**. This is like a simple prayer or blessing. Some people use a **mala** (a string of beads) to keep count of the times they have said the mantra. Monks or priests make the offerings and chant scriptures and words like these:

'In reverence to the Buddha we offer incense
Incense whose fragrance fills the air
The fragrance of the perfect life, sweeter than incense
Spreads in all directions throughout the world.'

In Theravada shrines the image is of Gotama Buddha. In Mahayana shrines it might be the Buddha or any other buddha or **bodhisattva** (A). A bodhisattva is a being who puts off entry into Nibbana to help others in the world.

Symbols

Tibetan centres often have **thankas**. These are paintings of buddhas and religious symbols. There might be prayer flags and wheels (**B**) with mantras written on them. Turning the wheel is like saying the mantra.

Some Buddhist centres have sand and rock gardens. The sand is raked into a simple pattern (**C**). Beautiful gardens in Buddhist centres remind Buddhists of the changes in life.

New words

incense   mantra   mala   bodhisattva   thankas

THINGS TO DO

1 Explain how the body, speech and mind are each involved in offering devotion.

2 Explain what you think the devotional words opposite about offering incense mean.

3 Make a leaflet which tells people about Buddhist shrines and places of meditation.

4 When prayer wheels are turned it is as if the words on them are being sent out into the world. Many people believe words are very powerful. How might this be true? Do you believe thoughts have power? What do you think might be meant by 'the power of positive thought'? Discuss your ideas in class.

C A Buddhist sand and rock garden

Meditation

Learning to meditate is important to Buddhists. It helps with two parts of the Eightfold Path: Right mindfulness or awareness and Right concentration (see page 37). This involves training the mind to be calm and controlled.

Breathing

There are several kinds of Buddhist meditation. One form centres on the person's breathing. For this the Buddha said people should sit cross-legged with a straight back. Sitting up straight is the most important thing so people can do this seated in a chair (**A**). Then Buddhists concentrate on their breathing. They do not try to change it but just be aware of it.

B Japanese Buddhist tea ceremony

At first this is difficult because a person's thoughts jump from one thing to another. After much practice it is possible to be aware only of breathing. Many Buddhists say doing this makes them feel refreshed.

Discussion question

Why do you think sitting upright is important for this form of meditation? It is also important not to be stiff or tense. Why?

Awareness

In other kinds of meditation people become very aware and mindful of anything and everything they do. This form of meditation can be done anywhere and anytime. It makes people very aware of the present moment rather than thinking of the past or planning for the future.

People have to concentrate on whatever it is they are doing but not on themselves. A tea ceremony is used by some Japanese

A It is possible to meditate sitting in a chair

C Japanese flower arranging (ikebana)

Buddhists (**B**). Those who do this must focus on the tea and how it is prepared. They must not focus on what *they* are doing with it. Flower arranging (ikebana) (**C**), archery and walking are other activities which some Buddhists use as ways of meditating.

Feelings

Another kind of meditation concentrates on feelings. It is a way of overcoming feelings like anger and envy. Buddhists try to look at what started the feelings, the effect they are having and how they die away. They are not trying to judge whether the feelings are good or bad. It is about being aware of what is really happening. The Buddha taught:

'The one who protects his mind from greed, anger and foolishness, is the one who enjoys real and lasting peace.'

THINGS TO DO

1 If you were able to interview a Buddhist about their meditation practice, what questions would you ask and why?

2 Write an article for a magazine about different kinds of Buddhist meditation.

3 Do you agree with the Buddha that we often think more about the past or the future than we do about the present? Try to give examples to back up your view. Discuss this in class.

4 Try to still your mind with a breathing meditation. Try sitting up straight without being tense. Place your hands comfortably in your lap. You might like to close your eyes. Try to concentrate on your breathing. Afterwards discuss how you felt.

Christian belief in God: Three in one

The Trinity

Christians believe in one God. They believe he is so great no one can understand him fully. However, they say it is possible for God to be a personal friend.

A Christian way of understanding God is to speak of him as three in one. God is understood to be Father, Son and Holy Spirit (**A**). This belief is called the Trinity. Father, Son and Holy Spirit are not three separate beings. They are different ways of God making himself known to people (**B**).

A Christians believe God is three in one

What Christians believe

From the early times of Christianity, followers thought it was important to be clear about their main beliefs. **Creeds** were drawn up to say what beliefs all Christians shared. The **Nicene Creed** is still used in many churches. It sets out beliefs about the Trinity as shown in this extract:

> 'We believe in one God,
> the Father, the almighty,
> maker of heaven and earth …
> We believe in one Lord, Jesus Christ,
> the only Son of God …
> of one Being with the Father …
> … We believe in the Holy Spirit,
> the Lord, the giver of life,
> who proceeds from the Father and the Son
> …

Discussion question

What do you think are the advantages and difficulties for Christians of having a statement of their main beliefs?

Father, Son and Holy Spirit

As the Father, God is believed to be creator of all things. This does not mean that all Christians believe he made the world in six days, as described in the beginning of the Bible. Many believe the story is not literally true. However, they say it shows the creative power of God.

God the Son is the second part of the Trinity. Christians believe that God showed himself in the person of Jesus. This is because he loved the world. Many believe Jesus was actually the Son of God. Others believe the stories show Jesus was a man filled with the spirit and goodness

B The Triangular Lodge in Rushton, Northamptonshire is a symbol of the Trinity

of God. He was in some way God and man together.

The Holy Spirit is seen as God's presence in people and in the world. He is believed to bring comfort and inspiration to individual believers and the Christian community.

New words

Creeds   Nicene Creed

THINGS TO DO

1 What impressions do pictures **A** and **B** create of the Trinity? Do they help you understand the Trinity? Give reasons for your answers.

2 Design a symbol, picture or collage of the Christian idea of the Trinity.

3 Read the extract from the Nicene Creed on page 48. What does it tell you Christians believe about the Trinity? Discuss your ideas in a group.

4 Putting together a statement of beliefs that everyone agrees on is not always easy. Work in a group to see if you can draw up a short list of beliefs about life which you all agree on. How easy is it for the whole class to agree a list?

The Bible

One of the ways Christians learn about their religion and its teachings is by reading the **Bible** (A). The Bible is a collection of books which make up the scriptures of Christianity. There are two main sections.

The Old Testament

The larger section contains writings from Jewish scriptures. This is because the first Christians were Jewish. It was written in Hebrew. This part of the Christian Bible became known at the **Old Testament.**

B The New Testament books were first written in Greek

The New Testament

The other section, called the **New Testament**, contains writings by Christians. Most were first written in Greek (**B**). Many would say the most important of these are the **Gospels**. These were written to get people to believe Jesus Christ was God. They tell of his life and teachings.

In the New Testament there are also letters from St Paul and other church leaders. These give guidance and encouragement for members of the Church. Another book called the Acts of the Apostles tells the story of the early Christian Church.

The canon of scripture

It was not until the fourth century CE that Christians decided what would be in the Bible. The writings included are known as the **canon** of scripture.

The Bible is very important for Christians. They read it to find out what God taught through the prophets and the life of Jesus.

A Christians learn about their religion through the Bible

Discussion question

In what ways do you think the Bible is helpful to Christians?

The loaves and fishes

A large crowd had followed Jesus and his disciples. In the evening the disciples suggested Jesus should send the people away to get something to eat. Jesus said, 'You yourselves give them something to eat.' They answered, 'All we have are five loaves and two fish.' There were about 5000 people there. Jesus told his disciples to get the people to sit down. He thanked God for the loaves and fish, broke them and gave them to the disciples to give out. Everyone ate and had enough.

Understanding the Bible

Some Christians believe the Bible is the actual Word of God. They claim the words in the Bible came directly from God and were written down exactly as they were given. Many more, however, believe the Bible contains the Word of God. This means the writers were inspired by God. They wrote in their own words and also used the ideas of their times. Many parts of the Bible are believed to teach important messages. But many Christians say some advice in the Bible is out of date.

THINGS TO DO

1 The Bible is a very important book for Christians. It helps them to understand life and how they should live. Think of some books you have found helpful. Explain how they were helpful to you.

2 Christians agreed on what should go in the Bible to make sure it taught the Christian message correctly. Each day different newspapers report slightly different versions of the same stories. What are the advantages and disadvantages of reading only one version of news stories? Is it important that we try to get the most accurate information?

3 In this unit you have found out about different parts of the Bible. Make a list of the different parts of the Bible you have read about. Beside each one write what you have learnt about it.

4 Read the story of the loaves and fish in the box at the top of this page or in Mark 6:30-44. Some say that Jesus multiplied the bread and fishes. Others say it is a story about sharing. In groups discuss what you think the message might be.

New words

Bible   Old Testament
New Testament   Gospels   canon

Jesus

Christians believe that God showed himself in the world in the life of Jesus. In the Gospels Jesus is shown as a teacher, a healer and a friend to people from all walks of life.

Jesus the healer

Jesus showed the love of God in his care for others. There are many stories of him healing the sick. One was about the blind man called Bartimaeus who called to Jesus as he walked along the road. He asked Jesus to heal him. Jesus told him his faith had made him well. At once Bartimaeus was able to see (**A**).

Jesus the friend

Jesus was also concerned about people who were unpopular. Zacchaeus was a tax collector. When Jesus visited Jericho, Zacchaeus climbed a tree so he would be able to see him (**B**). Jesus saw him and told him to get down so he could stay in his house. People criticized Jesus for being friendly with such a man.

A Jesus healed blind Bartimaeus

B People criticized Jesus for being friendly towards Zacchaeus

Luke's Gospel describes how Zacchaeus changed because of his meeting with Jesus. He gave money to the poor and repaid those he had cheated.

Discussion question

Who are the unpopular people of our time and society?

Christians today believe that Jesus can still change lives. When people read about him in the Bible they may be inspired to follow the Christian way. They try to practise what Jesus taught. In this way they can show the presence of God in the world. They help to change the lives of others.

Jesus the teacher

In Matthew's Gospel Jesus said:

'Do not judge others…for God will judge you in the same way as you judge others.'
(Matthew 7:1-2)

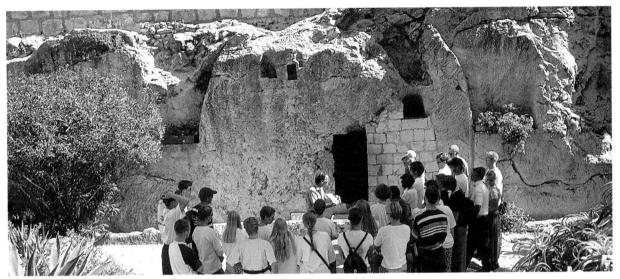

C The garden tomb in Israel. Some believe this is where Jesus' body was laid and where he came back to life

He said the two greatest commandments were:

'Love the Lord your God with all your heart, with all your soul, and with all your mind.'
(Matthew 22:37)

'Love your neighbour as you love yourself.'
(Matthew 22:39)

Those who put these teachings into practice can change the lives of people they meet just as Jesus did.

Christians believe Jesus came back to life after he had been crucified (**C**). He showed there is life after death. Christians believe they will live a spiritual life with God when their earthly lives end.

THINGS TO DO

1 What do you think Jesus meant when he told people not to judge others? Why might it be good or difficult for people to follow this advice? Write a short story about judging, or not judging, others.

2 The ideal Christian life is sometimes described as the **Kingdom of God**. Some people think this is a new life Christians have after the end of their earthly lives. Others believe they can be part of the Kingdom of God during this life. What do you think?

3 Jesus said, 'Love your neighbour as you love yourself.' Write or draw what you think he meant about:

- loving ourselves
- loving our neighbours as we love ourselves.

4 Draw a diagram which shows how Jesus was:

- a teacher
- a healer
- a friend.

> **New word**
>
> Kingdom of God

26 The Church

The early days

After Jesus left the earth and went to heaven, his followers carried on his teaching. As these early followers grew old and died, Christians had to learn from the books. These became the New Testament.

As the religion spread, many who became Christians could not read the Bible. Gradually people were specially trained to understand the Bible and to lead worship. These became the leaders of the Church. Ordinary Christians looked to church leaders to teach them about their religion.

Different Christian denominations

The Church grew in different ways. Groups formed into denominations. Each expressed its faith in its own way. The denomination with the largest number of members is the **Roman Catholic Church**.

Roman Catholics believe one of Jesus' disciples, Peter, was the first **pope**. This is the name for the head of the Roman Catholic church (**A**). They believe that the true beliefs of Christianity have been passed on from pope to pope through the years. This means the pope can decide on new teachings of the Roman Catholic church on his own. However, he has many **cardinals, bishops** and **priests** to help him.

Some other denominations, such as the **Orthodox churches** and the **Church of England**, also have bishops and priests or **vicars** (**B**). Leaders of other denominations are called **ministers** or **elders**.

A Pope John Paul II, the head of the Roman Catholic Church

All these leaders have studied the Bible and the teachings of their church very carefully.

They have been trained to lead worship and guide other people to understand the Christian faith.

Discussion question

Some Christian groups do not have leaders. Anyone can help to lead worship. What do you think might be the good things and the difficulties of this?

In 1948 the World Council of Churches was set up. It says although there are differences between denominations they are all part of the Church of Christ.

B Church leaders in a procession

New words

Roman Catholic Church   pope
cardinals   bishops   priests
Orthodox churches   Church of England
vicars   ministers   elders

C The symbol of the World Council of Churches

THINGS TO DO

1 Look at the photos of church leaders (**A** and **B**). They often stand out because of the clothes they wear. What are the advantages and disadvantages of this for them and members of their congregations?

2 What do you think are the advantages and disadvantages of different churches:
   • remaining separate
   • coming together?

3 Look at the symbol of the World Council of Churches (**C**). Try to explain what it means. (Oikoumene means 'one world'.)

4 Church leaders help people to understand Christian beliefs and teachings. Can you think of others who guide people in their lives and beliefs? Explain how they do this. When might an expert be able to help you?

The Christian family at worship

The Church

The word 'church' can mean all Christians. It can mean particular groups of Christians, for example the **Methodists**. It is also a building where Christians meet.

There are many different kinds of church. By looking at different buildings we can learn about the ways in which Christians express their faith.

The first followers of Jesus met wherever they could, often in people's houses. A church does not need to be anything special. Some Christians today meet in each others' homes to pray. Such groups are called house churches. The worship is informal and no priest is involved.

A The Bible is often placed on a lectern for reading

B An Orthodox priest carries the Bible in an Easter procession

The Bible

The Bible is used in Christian worship. It has been translated into most languages.

In **Anglican** and Roman Catholic services there are readings from the Old and New Testaments. The Bible is often placed on a **lectern** (**A**). When the Gospel is read the congregation stands up as a sign of respect. In Orthodox churches, the Bible is often beautifully bound. It is sometimes carried in processions (**B**).

In many churches the service is based on the Bible reading. Hymns and prayers are on the same theme. The preacher's talk may be based on it. He or she tries to explain what the reading means for people today. The preacher may stand in a pulpit (**C**). This is raised so people can see the speaker and understand that his or her teaching is important.

New words

Methodists   Anglican   lectern

Discussion question

When you have read the next paragraph, say what you think is meant by the words, 'give themselves to Christ'.

The Holy Spirit

Christians believe that the Holy Spirit is present when they meet together for worship. Some say the Holy Spirit makes them want to give themselves to Christ.

THINGS TO DO

1 Standing up is often a sign of respect. When might people do this?

2 Look at the photo of the lectern (**A**). It is made in the shape of an eagle with outstretched wings standing on a sphere. What do you think this means?

3 Using the photos in this unit to help you, write an article about the importance of the Bible in Christian worship. Unit 24 will also help you.

4 Try to find out what sorts of churches there are in the area around your school and some information about them. You could make a display of your findings.

C Preaching is often done from the pulpit so that everyone can see the speaker

28 Bread and wine

Jesus' last supper

The sharing of bread and wine is an important way of worshipping in many denominations. Before he was arrested, Jesus had a meal with his disciples (**A**). Many believe this was the Jewish **Passover** meal. At the supper, he broke a piece of bread and gave it to his disciples to eat. He also poured some wine and gave it to them to drink. He said they should do this to remember him.

Sharing bread and wine

Different churches share bread and wine in different ways. In most, people prepare themselves with prayers and readings. They ask God to forgive their wrongdoings, selfishness and unkindness. Then the bread and wine are blessed.

Discussion question

Why do you think people believe it is important to prepare themselves in this kind of way?

These churches, in different ways, believe that Christ somehow becomes present in the bread and wine. How this happens is a mystery which cannot be fully explained.

The Roman Catholic service is called **Mass**. Anglicans call it **Holy Communion** or Eucharist. As priests give the bread they say, 'The body of Christ'. With the wine they say, ' The blood of Christ'.

A Jesus sharing his last meal with his disciples before he was arrested

B A Greek Orthodox priest giving bread and wine on a spoon as part of the Liturgy

Everyone shares one cup called a **chalice**.

The Orthodox church calls the service the **Liturgy**. People receive bread and wine together on a spoon (**B**).

In all three churches, this is a reminder of Jesus' death. The sharing of bread and wine takes place at least once a week (**C**).

In other denominations, including the **Baptist** and Methodist churches, this sharing may happen only once a month.

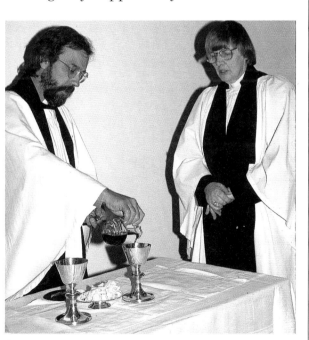

C Bread and wine being prepared

Each person has their own cup of wine or grape juice. The service helps people remember Jesus' last supper. Some Christian groups share bread and wine in their own homes.

Some groups, for example the **Society of Friends** and the **Salvation Army**, do not have this service.

New words

Passover   Mass   Holy Communion
chalice   Liturgy   Baptist
Society of Friends   Salvation Army
sacraments

THINGS TO DO

1 In the Orthodox, Anglican and Roman Catholic churches, sharing of bread and wine is one of the **sacraments**. These churches believe God works through sacraments. Design a poster to explain the meaning of the bread and wine in these churches.

2 Design a short Christian service. Choose or write prayers, hymns and readings on the theme of forgiveness.

3 The Society of Friends and the Salvation Army say that every shared meal is important. Why is sharing food with someone meaningful? How is it different from eating alone? When do people share meals?

4 If your class were to have a friendship meal once a week with everyone bringing something, what problems might arise? How could they be sorted out? What good things might come from such a meal?

Living Christianity

Teaching children

Christians try to follow the example of Jesus. Christian parents try to set a good example. They want their children to know about Jesus. They teach them to pray. Some families thank God for his goodness at mealtimes (**A**).

Discussion question

What do you think it means for Christian parents to set a good example?

Families may study the Bible and pray together. Many believers read their Bible every day. Its teachings guide them.

A At mealtimes some families thank God for his goodness

Going to church

Christians worship with others in churches. Children may go to a Sunday school where they are taught more about the faith. People help the church in many ways. They might serve coffee after the service, run a creche or help with the Sunday school or youth club. Others hold Bible study or prayer groups in their homes.

Prayer

Prayer is very important for Christians. This is the main way they communicate with God. Christians believe they can listen to God as well as speak to him. Very few ever expect to hear a voice speaking aloud to them. When they pray they often find they can understand something better and feel they know what to do.

There are different kinds of prayer. Christians praise God for his greatness and also thank him for all he has done. Sometimes they want to say sorry. They confess what they have done and ask for forgiveness. This often helps them put right what they have done wrong and make a new start. Christians often ask for God's help for themselves and others.

Some people ask whether prayers are answered. Christians say prayers can be answered in many ways. For example, someone may pray for a sick friend to be healed. The friend may seem to recover miraculously. Or she may find extra strength to cope because she knows that people care enough to pray for her. Prayer often shows Christians how they can help themselves.

B Standing to pray

C Some people sit for prayer

The Lord's Prayer

'Our Father in heaven,
hallowed be your name,
your kingdom come,
your will be done,
on earth as in heaven.
Give us today our daily
bread.
Forgive us our sins
as we forgive those who sin
against us.
Lead us not into temptation
but deliver us from evil.
For the kingdom, the power,
and the glory are yours,
now and forever. Amen.'

THINGS TO DO

1 Christians can stand, sit or kneel to pray (**B** and **C**). Sometimes they close their eyes. Prayers might be spoken or silent. What do you think are the good points of all these ways of praying? Write up your thought with pictures.

2 Read the Lord's Prayer in the box on the left. It contains praise, thanksgiving, confession and asking. Draw a chart with four columns. Divide up the Lord's Prayer into praise, thanksgiving, confession and asking and put each part in a separate column. Write your own prayer which includes all four kinds of prayer.

3 Some churches have prayer lists. People write down what they want others to pray about. What sort of things would you expect to find included? What might you choose to add and why?

4 Most Christians want to pass their faith on to their children. Imagine you are a parent. What ideas and beliefs are important enough to you for you to want to pass them on to your children? How do you think parents feel if their children reject their beliefs and follow other directions?

30

Faith and conviction

Most Christians put their faith into practice in ordinary lives.

Monastic life

A few Christians choose to dedicate their whole lives to God and join a **monastic order** of **monks** or **nuns**. They make vows, or promises, of poverty, chastity and obedience. This means they have no, or very few, personal possessions. They will not marry or have sexual relationships. Their lives are lived in obedience to God.

Some live entirely within their communities and spend most of their time in prayer and study. Members of other orders work in society. This is often in education, health care and in organizations which help the poor and underprivileged. These Christians try to improve their own spiritual lives. They also believe they help the world with their prayers and work (**A**).

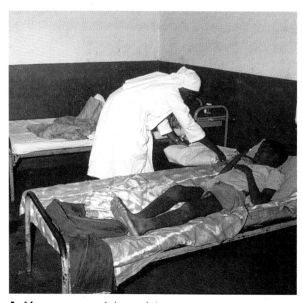

A Many nuns work in society

Helping the needy

Many Christians say that Jesus spoke out against unfairness, poverty, greed and selfishness. Christians remember a passage from Luke's gospel (Luke 4:18). It says God chose Jesus to bring good news to the poor, help free captives and help the blind to see.

Fighting unfairness

Many believe they should also take a stand against unfairness. A story in Matthew's gospel (25:31-46) makes them think about this. The story tells of people being judged by whether they have fed the hungry, given a drink to the thirsty, received strangers into their homes, clothed the naked, taken care of the sick and visited those in prison. Jesus said:

'…whenever you did this for one of the least important of these brothers of mine you did it for me! …whenever you refused to help one of these least important ones, you refused to help me.'

Liberation Theology

A Christian movement known as **Liberation Theology** started in South America to help those who are treated unfairly.

Discussion question

Do you think people have a responsibility to care for those who are less fortunate?

People continue this work all over the world. Archbishop Desmond Tutu, for example, spoke out about the evil of apartheid in South Africa (**B**).
In Britain, the Church of England has spoken out in support of the needy. Its 1986 report, 'Faith in the City', criticized government policies of the time (**C**).
Many Christians believe these actions continue the work of Jesus in the world.

B Archbishop Desmond Tutu spoke out against apartheid in South Africa

New words

monastic order   monks   nuns
Liberation Theology

C The Church of England published a report. It said there should be help for the needy

THINGS TO DO

1 Discuss the differences between the poverty of a monastic life and the poverty forced upon people who are in need.

2 Some Christians work for improvements in society. What parts of our society do you think need to be improved and how? Create a poster to illustrate your ideas.

3 Try to find out about how Christian groups in your area help in the community. Record the information on a chart.

4 This and other chapters on Christianity in this book show that there are many ways of being a Christian. Explain some of these ways in a diagram or short magazine article.

31

Islam: The word of Allah

Muslims believe that **Allah** (God) has given humankind guidance on how to live. He has sent messengers and **prophets** in every age. Muslims believe that the final and most perfect revelation of the word of Allah is contained in the **Qur'an** (A).

Muhammad

Muslims believe that every single word of the Quran is the word of Allah. For Muslims it has the highest authority. The words were revealed to the Prophet **Muhammad** by the angel **Jibril**.

Muhammad repeated them to his followers. Every word was carefully kept and written down. Muslims believe that no word has been changed.

B The beautiful and unique text of the Qur'an

According to the Qur'an, people can choose how to live. They can follow their own crooked way in life or they can follow the straight path that leads to peace. This is what the Qur'an says:

> 'And He commands you saying:
> This is my straight path, so follow it. Do not follow other paths which will separate you from His path.'
>
> (6:153)

Discussion question

What path in life do you follow? Do any rules or teachings guide it?

Recitation

The word Qur'an means 'recitation'. In other words something that is recited or said out loud. Its teachings cover every aspect of life. How to pray, what food to eat, how to run a business, how to govern a country. The Qur'an is written in **Arabic** (B). Its poetry is very beautiful. Muslims believe that when it is recited the sound of the language draws the listener to Allah. The text of the Qur'an is divided into chapters called **surahs**. These are also divided into verses.

A A Muslim child reading from the Qur'an

Muslim children start to read the Qur'an in Arabic when they are very young (**B**). Some Muslims learn to recite the whole Qur'an from memory. A Muslim who can do this is called **hafiz**. The Qur'an is handled with great care. Muslims always wash before they open the pages.

New words

Allah   prophets   Qur'an
Muhammad   Jibril   Arabic   surahs
hafiz

THINGS TO DO

1 Write three sentences explaining why the Qur'an is so special for Muslims.

2 Imagine your school library has been given a copy of the Qur'an. Write a set of guidelines for pupils about how to handle this very special book with care.

3 Listen to someone reciting the words of the Qur'an. A selection of readings can be heard in *The Life of the Last Prophet* by Yusuf Islam, Mountain of Light Productions, P.O. Box 7404, London N7.

4 People say, 'Do your own thing. Live your own life!' Is this helpful? What problems arise when everyone follows their own way in life? Write an article for a newspaper in answer to this problem.

C Children learn to read the Qur'an from an early age

32

Three key beliefs

The three most important beliefs in Islam are **tawhid** (Oneness of Allah), **risalah** (prophethood) and **akhirah** (life after death).

Tawhid

Muslims believe in One God Allah. Allah is unique. There is none like him. The belief in the Oneness of Allah is called tawhid. Allah is invisible and cannot be shown in any shape or form. Although Allah cannot be seen he can be described in terms of his beautiful names (**A**). For example, Allah is 'All-Merciful' and 'All-Holy'. Muslims recite the ninety-nine beautiful names of Allah to remember him (**B**).

Meditating on the beautiful names of Allah

B A Muslim recites the ninety-nine beautiful names of Allah

is important to **Sufis**. Sufis are Muslims who believe that the Oneness of Allah can be experienced in all aspects of life. It means seeing Allah in all creation (**C**).

Risalah

According to the Qur'an, Allah has given his guidance to humankind. He did this through his prophets and messengers. This way that Allah communicated with humans is called risalah.

Discussion question

A prophet is sometimes called a messenger. Do you think this is a helpful description?

A The ninety-nine beautiful names of Allah

The prophets

Muslims accept the same prophets as in the Jewish and Christian scriptures. They say Jesus was a prophet. They do not believe he was the Son of God. Muslims believe it is wrong to say that God had a son. It is a wrong belief because it suggests that Allah is more than One. Wrong belief is called **shirk**.

Muslims believe that Muhammad was the last of the prophets. Allah revealed the words of the Qur'an to him. Muhammad was a very good person and Muslims try to follow his example. But they do not regard him as divine or equal to Allah.

Akhirah

Belief in life after death is called akhirah. Muslims believe that there will be a **Day of Judgement**. Everyone will be called by Allah and judged according to their actions. Those who have followed the teachings of Allah will be rewarded in **Paradise**. Those who have gone against the will of Allah will be punished.

THINGS TO DO

1 Prepare a set of six questions on the key beliefs in Islam. Swap your work with a partner.

2 Divide a page in two. On one side list the Muslim beliefs about life after death. On the other side write down three beliefs about life after death that are different from the Muslim beliefs. Say which you agree with and why.

3 If there was another prophet today what do you think their message would be to the world? Write your answer as a poem or a news article.

4 In what way do you think the belief in life after death affects the way a person lives this life? Write down three ideas.

New words

tawhid   risalah   akhirah   Sufi
shirk   Day of Judgement   Paradise

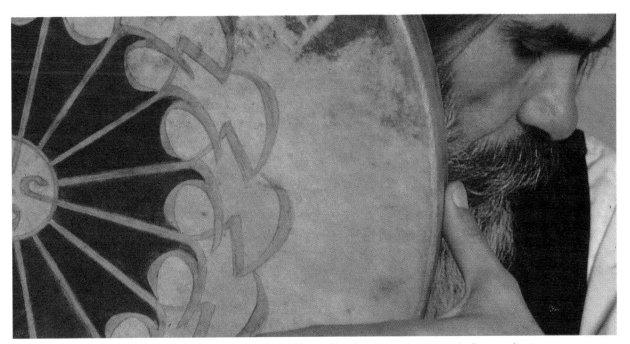

C The Sufi tradition emphasizes the oneness of all things. This is shown in its symbolism and art

33

Good examples

Muhammad is an example for Muslims to follow. The collected sayings and stories from the life of Muhammad were carefully recorded and passed on. They are contained in the **Hadith** which means information or 'news'. The Hadith helps Muslims to work out the meaning of the Qur'an. For example, the Qur'an tells Muslims to perform **salah**. The Hadith tells Muslims how Muhammad prayed. It gives information on how to follow the Qur'an.

Stories in the Hadith

Muslim children learn the stories in the Hadith (**A**). This is one for adults and children:

> A man once asked the Prophet, '…messenger of Allah! Who deserves the best care from me?' The Prophet said, 'Your mother!' The man asked, 'Who then?' The Prophet said, 'Your mother.' The man asked once again. The Prophet said again, 'Your mother.'
>
> (Hadith)

Discussion question

What does this story from the Hadith tell you about the place of women in Islam?

A Muslim children study the Hadith at Madrasah

Sunni and Shi'ah

There are two main groups of Muslims, the **Sunni** and the **Shi'ah**. They differ very little in belief and practice. They do have different views about who was the right person to succeed Muhammad. Sunni Muslims believe that Abu Bakr, Muhammad's closest friend, was the successor or Khalifah.

Shi'ah Muslims have a different view. Muhammad's daughter, Fatimah, had five children. Shi'ah Muslims believe her son, Husain, is the successor to the Prophet. Husain was murdered when he was fighting to protect the weak. Many Muslims remember Husain as an example of self-sacrifice and faith (**B**).

B Shi'ah Muslims re-enacting the martyrdom of Husain

New words
Hadith   salah   Sunni   Shi'ah

THINGS TO DO

1 Look at these sentences. Write out the ones that are true:

   a) The Hadith contains the sayings of Muhammad.

   b) Stories about Muhammad were kept and written down.

   c) The word Hadith means prayers.

   d) Muslims use the Hadith to help them understand the Qur'an.

2 Design a cover for the Hadith. Why should you avoid using pictures of the Prophet? What could you use instead?

3 In your own words, write three sentences about Muhammad's wife, Khadijah.

4 The story of Husain is acted out each year by Shi'ah Muslims. Which good person do you think should be remembered every year? Explain your answer in full sentences.

Khadijah

Muslims follow the example of the Prophet. His wife, Khadijah, is a model for women to follow. It was Khadijah who proposed to Muhammad. They married and had two sons and four daughters. Khadijah was the first to accept that Muhammad was a prophet with a message from Allah. Her faith is an example to others.

34

Belief in action

In Islam the word **ibadah** means belief or faith put into action. Muslims have five ways of putting faith into action. These are the Five Pillars of Islam.

Shahadah

The first pillar is **shahadah**. This is a statement of faith. It says what a Muslim believes in:

> 'I bear witness that there is no God except Allah, Muhammad is the messenger of Allah.'

Salah

The second pillar is salah. This is prayer five times a day (**A**). Of course Muslims can pray as often as they want but there are five set prayers.

Sawm

The third pillar is **sawm** or fasting. Muslims must fast during the month of **Ramadan**. They go without food or water during the hours of daylight. Sawm involves the whole person: ears, eyes, heart and hands must all avoid evil. Fasting helps Muslims to build up the strength to overcome evil and temptation. Sawm is an act of self-sacrifice.

Zakah

Zakah is the fourth pillar of Islam. Every Muslim must give two and a half per cent of their savings to the poor and needy. In this way they help in Allah's plan to provide for all in the community. Giving to the poor stops people from being too greedy and selfish. Like fasting, zakah is an act of self-sacrifice.

Discussion question

Why do you think that buying lottery tickets cannot count as zakah?

A Muslim at prayer

B The Ka'bah at Makkah which pilgrims face as they pray to Allah

Hajj

The last pillar of Islam is **hajj**. This is the pilgrimage to **Makkah** (**B**). Muslims must try to go to the holy city at least once in their lifetime.

New words

ibadah	shahadah	sawm
Ramadan	zakah	hajj	Makkah

THINGS TO DO

1 Write two sentences about each of the Five Pillars of Islam.

2 Your belief must show in your actions. Draw a cartoon to illustrate this statement.

3 Describe or draw what is happening in photo **A** and in photo **B**. Say which of the five pillars are shown in these photos.

4 The Five Pillars help Muslims to build their life around their faith. What are the beliefs and practices that hold your life together? Write down two examples of beliefs that are important to you. Then write two examples of commitments/things you do regularly that are important in your life.

35 Daily prayer

Salah involves both words and actions. This helps to focus the body and mind on Allah during prayer. Life is busy and it is hard to concentrate on prayer.

The adhan

Muslims are called to pray five times a day – early morning, noon, mid-afternoon, at sunset and last thing at night. The times are shown in the **mosque**.

The **adhan** or call to prayer reminds Muslims when it is time for salah. The **mu'adhin** calls the adhan from the **minaret** at the mosque.

Discussion question
Sometimes salah can be hard to do regularly. Why?

Preparation

Muslims remove their shoes before prayer. They wash in preparation for salah. This is called **wudu** (A). They wash their feet, hands, face, mouth, nose and ears. As they do this they remember the things they have done wrong and prepare to stand before Allah.

Rak'ah

Salah is made up of units of prayer. Each unit is called a **rak'ah**. It involves both words and actions. It begins with the words 'God is Great'.

Where to pray

Muslims can pray at home or wherever they are at the set time for prayer. All they

A Muslims performing wudu in preparation for salah

B The prayer positions express total submission to Allah

need is a clean place to **prostrate** themselves. Muslims are encouraged to pray at the mosque if they can. Praying together with others is a good thing. Worshippers stand shoulder to shoulder facing Makkah. This is a sign of equality.

At the mosque the **imam** leads the prayers. The voices together and the movements of the prayers all help to express the feeling of unity and obedience to the will of Allah (**B**).

Personal prayers

After the set prayers many Muslims say their own personal prayers called **du'a** (**C**). They may ask forgiveness for something they have done wrong. They may ask Allah to look after their loved ones.

New words

mosque adhan mu'adhin minaret
wudu rak'ah prostrate imam du'a

C The end of salah is often the time for personal prayers

36

Home and family

Muslims believe that the family is the basis for a good society. For most children, home is the place where the teachings of Islam are first learnt. Children follow the example of their parents and learn the pattern of salah (**A**).

Different roles

According to the Qur'an, men and women have different roles in the home and in life. The mother has the responsibility for bringing up the children. She must teach them the faith of Islam. That does not mean that Muslim women cannot go out to work. In fact, if they do, they may keep their earnings for themselves.

It is the responsibility of the father to provide the financial support for his wife and family. Children must respect their elders. Parents must be reasonable with their children. Elderly relatives are cared for in the family home.

Modest dress

The Qur'an requires all Muslims to dress

A Children learn salah from the example of their parents

B Muhammad told his followers they should share food

modestly. Women must cover their body except for face and hands when they are outside the family home. In the mosque men wear a cap or hat and women cover their hair.

Food that is allowed

The Qur'an gives guidance for eating and preparing food. It forbids alcohol. It also forbids the following foods: pork, meat-eating animals, carrion (that is animals that have died naturally), and animals that were killed without the name of Allah said over them. All meat must be drained of blood. Food that is fit to eat is called **halal**. Food that is forbidden is **haram**.

Discussion question

Everyone has their own rules about what they can and cannot eat. What are your rules?

Giving thanks and sharing

Muhammad told his followers that they should share their food with others (**B**). At the festival of **Id-ul-Adha** every family that can afford it sacrifices an animal. They share the meat with the poor.

New words

halal   haram   Id-ul-Adha

THINGS TO DO

1 Write down three things that happen in a Muslim home that make it different from a non-Muslim home. What things do you think would be the same in both?

2 Design a leaflet to explain Muslim food laws for non-Muslims going to a Muslim country.

3 Write a story in which a Muslim explains to a non-Muslim friend about what to wear when going to the mosque.

4 What do you think makes a home a special place?

37

Place of prostration

The word mosque means a place of prostration. In the UK some mosques are converted houses. Many are now purpose-built with a dome and minaret (**A**). The minaret is the tower from where the call to prayer is given.

Inside the mosque

At the mosque there is always a place to wash before prayer. There is a prayer hall (**B**). It has no seating but the floor is carpeted. One wall, called the Qiblah, is marked with a niche or alcove to show the direction of Makkah. This is called the **mihrab**. In some mosques there is a gallery for the women to pray. Most Muslim women with children choose to pray at home. Some mosques encourage women to come to the mosque for prayer.

Imam

At every mosque there is an imam. He usually leads the prayers. The imam is chosen by the community. He is often a learned and respected man who knows the teachings of the Qur'an. He can offer advice and help to the community.

Community relations

The Qur'an teaches about the value of good relationships. Some mosques are community centres as well as places of worship. They may have facilities for a kitchen, a youth club and a reading room. Many mosques have classrooms where children study the Qur'an.

Discussion question

What things help to build good relations in a community?

A The traditional mosque has a minaret and dome

B Inside the mosque – the prayer hall

C At festival times Muslims have a sense of universal Ummah

Ummah

The Qur'an calls on Muslims to make a special effort to attend the mosque for Friday (**Jumu'ah**) prayers. Jumu'ah prayers are held just after midday. The imam gives a sermon. The mosque is full. Muslims feel close to other believers all over the world. Islam is a world-wide faith. The universal community of Muslims is called the **Ummah (C)**. At festival time many Muslims will seek out a large mosque to get this sense of the larger community.

Muslims pray facing Makkah. This helps to give a feeling of oneness and unity. Islam stresses the equality of all people. All are equal in the eyes of Allah.

New words

mihrab   Jumu'ah   Ummah

THINGS TO DO

1 Prepare a guidebook for a large mosque. Explain the purpose of the minaret, the mihrab and the fact that there are no seats.

2 Design a poster to encourage Muslims to come to the mosque to pray.

3 In your own words describe the meaning of the word Ummah. Say how Muslim prayer shows the Muslim idea of Ummah, a sense of being together as one.

4 A sense of community is important. Does your school have a sense of community? What could you do to improve the sense of community in your school?

38

The Sikh scriptures

The Sikh holy book is called the **Guru Granth Sahib**. It contains the words and teachings of Guru Nanak (1469–1539). Guru Nanak was the first of the ten Sikh **Gurus**. The Guru Granth Sahib also contains the works of the other Sikh Gurus. There are teachings from Hindu and Muslim holy men, too.

Discussion question

The Sikh holy book contains teachings from Muslims and Hindus as well as Sikhs. What does this tell you about the Sikh faith?

The first scriptures

Guru Arjan (1563–1606), the fifth Guru, put together the first collection of all the hymns of the Gurus. When the work was done he encouraged his fellow Sikhs to respect and listen to the words of the Gurus (**A**).

Guru Gobind Singh

The tenth Guru, Guru Gobind Singh (1666–1708), saw that there would be no living Guru after him. He told Sikhs that the Guru Granth Sahib would be like a living Guru for them. Guru Gobind Singh put together the final version of the Guru Granth Sahib. Today it is still given the honour due to a living Guru.

The words of the Gurus are called **Gurbani**. They are written in **Gurmukhi**.

A Guru Arjan reading the Guru Granth Sahib

B The chauri is waved over the Guru Granth Sahib

This was the script used by the Gurus to write **Punjabi**. The words of the Guru Granth Sahib are in poetry. They can be set to music. Each hymn is called a **shabad**.

At the gurdwara

At the Sikh place of worship called the **gurdwara**, the Guru Granth Sahib is read from a platform called a **takht**. On the takht is a stool called the **manji sahib**. This is covered and cushioned to hold the holy book. There is usually a canopy over the scriptures. When the holy book is open, a **chauri** is waved over the pages as a sign of respect (**B**).

The Guru Granth Sahib is read at all public acts of worship and celebrations. When it is not in use it is wrapped and carried to a bed where it rests in a room of its own (**C**).

Other Sikh scriptures

The Guru Granth Sahib is the sacred scripture of the Sikhs. There are also teachings of the tenth Guru in the **Dasam Granth**. The **Janamsakhis** are stories about the Gurus and many Sikhs read these too.

THINGS TO DO

1 Write three questions a visitor to the gurdwara might ask about the scriptures. Then write the answers a Sikh would give to your questions.

2 Look at picture **A**. In your own words and pictures explain who this is and what he was responsible for.

3 Do you remember the words of your teachers? Do you remember the words of pop songs? Why do you think that the Guru Granth Sahib works in the form of hymns and songs? Explain your answer.

4 Sikhs show respect to the Guru Granth Sahib. Describe what you see in the photos and say how respect is being shown to the Guru Granth Sahib.

New words

Guru Granth Sahib   Gurus   Gurbani
Gurmukhi   Punjabi   shabad
gurdwara   takht   manji sahib
chauri   Dasam Granth   Janamsakhis

C The Guru Granth Sahib is put to bed

39

Beliefs and teachings

Sikhs believe that there is only one God. They call God Waheguru. This means 'Wonderful Lord'. They also call God Sat Nam. This means the 'True Name'. There is no other like God. God is everywhere and in everything but has no form or features.

A personal God

The Guru Granth Sahib says God is a personal God who can be loved and worshipped (**A**). God breathes life into everyone. God's light is in each person's soul. It is this that gives humans the ability to judge good from evil.

Discussion question

How does the Sikh view of God compare with other ideas about God that you have studied?

Becoming close to God

Sikhs believe that the soul is eternal or never-ending. They believe we have all lived many lives including animal lives. When we are human, we can come close to God. We can do this by following the teachings of the Gurus. When we are united with God we are released from the cycle of rebirth. This release is called **mukti**.

Sikhs believe that all people are equal before God. This message is shown in the following story.

A God is a personal God who can be loved and worshipped

B Akbar the Great attending a langar at Ramgania Temple

Akbar the Great

There was once a king of India called Akbar the Great. Akbar planned to visit Guru Amar Das. He had heard that the Guru ran a **langar**, or community kitchen. Travellers, tramps and all who were hungry could come to eat. Everyone sat together on the floor to share a meal.

When the Sikhs heard that the king was coming they began to make special arrangements. But Guru Amar Das stopped them. The king was a human being like any other visitor. So when he arrived he had his meal with the common people and ate the simple food (**B**).

The king was so impressed he offered the Guru a royal grant. Guru Amar Das thanked him but said he could not accept. The langar must be run on the earnings of ordinary people. In that way everyone would feel equal.

New words
mukti   langar

THINGS TO DO

1 Write down these two headings:
   • Sikh beliefs about God
   • Sikh beliefs about people.
   Write four beliefs under each one.

2 Look at picture **B**. Describe what is in the picture. Draw it if you want. Explain the message of the story.

3 In your own words explain where Sikhs believe people get their sense of right and wrong. Give your own views.

4 Write a story that shows people are all equal.

40

Principles to live by

There are three principles that guide the way Sikhs live. **Nam Simran** or Nam Japna means remembering God at all times. **Kirat Karna** means earning an honest living. **Vand Chhakna** means sharing with others who do not have as much as you do.

Remembering God

Nam Simran is remembering God. There are many ways to do this. It may mean singing hymns of praise or meditating on the name of God. It may mean reciting the scriptures. In this way the heart and mind become filled with the awareness of God. Most people fill their minds with selfish desires. The aim of the Sikh is to be filled with the love of God.

Earning an honest living

Sikhs do not retreat to the forest to find God. Sikhs have to earn a living by honest means. They must be a part of the world of work, raise a family and run a home. God can be found in everyday life.

Discussion question

What work might be included in 'earning a living by honest means'? What work would not be included?

Guru Nanak and the bread

There was once a wealthy man called Malak Bhago. He made a fortune but he showed his workers no mercy and paid

A Guru Nanak squeezing the bread

B Sikhs share their resources – Vand Chhakna

poor wages. He invited Guru Nanak to eat at his house. Guru Nanak chose instead to eat at the house of Lalo, a poor carpenter.

Malak Bhago wanted to know why Guru Nanak preferred the poor man's bread to his fine meal. Guru Nanak put out his hand and asked for a piece of bread from his table. In the other hand he held the bread from Lalo's table. He then squeezed the two pieces of bread (**A**). From Malak Bhago's bread came drops of blood. From the poor man's bread came pure sweet milk. Then Guru Nanak said that he preferred bread that was earned by honest means to bread that was earned by the blood and suffering of others.

Sharing what you have

The third guiding principle for Sikhs is Vand Chhakna. This means sharing what you have with others (**B**).

THINGS TO DO

1 Write out the three principles that guide Sikh life. Write a sentence to explain each one.

2 Which of the three principles do you think would be hard to follow? Write your answer and give your reasons.

3 Design your own poster of Guru Nanak squeezing the bread. Explain what is happening in the picture.

4 Do you think that the story of Guru Nanak and the bread has meaning today? Explain why you think this message is still important.

New words

Nam Simran   Kirat Karna
Vand Chhakna

Worship

Sikhs believe that learning to put God first in life is hard. It is easier if you are a part of a community of people who are trying to do the same thing. The Sikh community is called the **sadhsangat**. The sadhsangat is where remembering God is taken seriously. Working and sharing with others is also important. There are no priests in the sadhsangat. All are equal. A **granthi** is chosen to lead the worship.

Discussion question

How does the life of the community around you affect the way you think and act?

The gurdwara

The life of the sadhsangat is centred around the gurdwara. Gurdwara means 'house to the Guru'. The main room of the gurdwara is the prayer hall. This is where the Guru Granth Sahib is read. Public worship takes place there. Sikhs wash before going to the gurdwara. They remove their shoes when they go in. They cover their heads in the presence of the Guru Granth Sahib. As they go up to the Guru Granth Sahib they bow and leave a gift of food or money.

Worship

Worship begins with **kirtan**. These are hymns from the Guru Granth Sahib. The worshippers stand for the prayer called the **ardas**. They remember God, the Gurus and those who have given their lives for the faith. They repeat God's name, Waheguru which means 'Wonderful

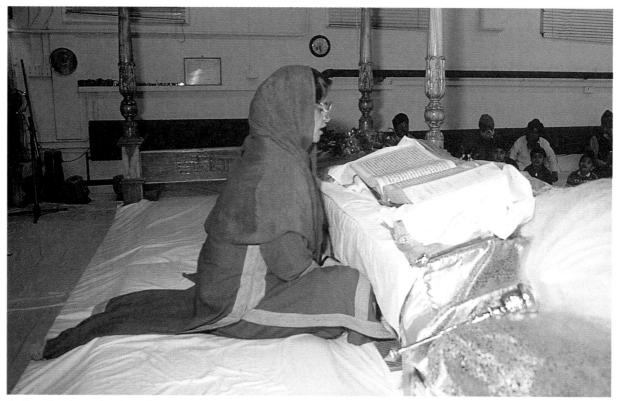

A Reading from the Guru Granth Sahib

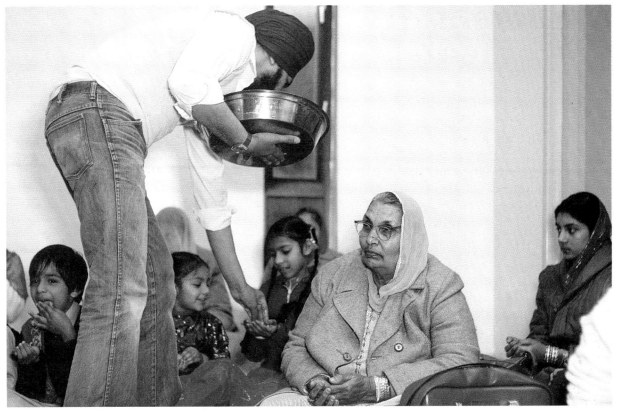

B The serving of karah parshad at the end of a service

Lord'. The prayer ends with a blessing for all humanity. The congregation sits for a reading from the Guru Granth Sahib (**A**). Below is a hymn from the Guru Granth Sahib:

'Repeat the Lord's name as the Guru commands us, for thus our sins are washed away; So greet every dawn with the words of the Guru and utter God's name through the length of the day.'

Karah parshad

At the end of the service there is **karah parshad**. This is a sweet mixture cooked from flour, butter, sugar and water. It is first offered before the Guru Granth Sahib. When it has been blessed it is served to everyone present (**B**).

THINGS TO DO

1 Write down the four stages in Sikh worship at the gurdwara.

2 Design a card or leaflet inviting Sikhs to visit their local gurdwara for worship.

3 Look at the words of the hymn from the Guru Granth Sahib. Choose one section to design a sticker for a Sikh car window.

4 Karah parshad is sweet. It represents God's blessing. What other good things in life do you think Sikhs might regard as blessings from God?

New words

sadhsangat   granthi   kirtan   ardas   karah parshad

42

Community meal

The Sikh community is like a large family. The worshippers pray together. They also cook and eat together (**B**). Every gurdwara has a langar or kitchen. After worship the congregation shares a community meal. This is also called langar.

A community meal

Everyone brings gifts of money and food when they come to worship. So the gurdwara is able to provide food free to visitors. Each week families volunteer to provide and prepare the community meal (**A**). The food is vegetarian. In this way everyone can eat the same food.

B Eating together in the langar

Langar is a way of showing that everyone is equal. In India the **caste system** used to divide people. People from different backgrounds could not eat together. The Sikh langar is a way of breaking down the barriers between the castes and between rich and poor.

A Sikhs preparing the langar in India

C Gurdwaras provide hospitals and schools and serve the local community. This gurdwara in Kenya, runs a large school

Discussion question

What kind of community events bring different people together ?

Serving the community

The gurdwara is open to everyone. It has always been a centre for serving the community. In India and Africa some gurdwaras provide hospitals and schools (**C**).

In the UK the gurdwara is a community centre. Many gurdwaras run a senior citizen's club and provide transport for the elderly. Some have a youth club and run classes for young people to learn to read and write Punjabi. Involving young people in the life of the sadhsangat is very important. It means that the Sikh traditions and values are passed on to the next generation.

The gurdwara is the centre for all religious occasions. Naming ceremonies, weddings and funerals all take place here. The gurdwara is managed by a committee chosen by the congregation. Committee members are volunteers who give up their time to serve the community.

New word

caste system

THINGS TO DO

1 Explain the Sikh word langar. Remember it has two meanings. In your own words say why langar is important in the Sikh community.

2 Design a poster calling for volunteers to help at the gurdwara. Draw some of different jobs they could do.

3 Imagine that you are taking a friend to the gurdwara. Write down four things that you think you should tell them about it before they go. Refer back to Unit 41 as well.

4 Write about an occasion when a meal helps to bring people together in friendship and trust. It can be real or imaginary.

43

In the home

Sikhs believe that God is found in daily life. There is no need to give up work or leave home to find God. Every action is an act of worship if it is done in God's name. No task is too low ar too unclean as long as it is honest and causes no harm.

A A Sikh family praying together at home

Prayer

Some Sikhs get up early in the morning when it is quiet. They shower before reciting their prayers (**A**). This prayer, the japji, is from the words of Guru Nanak:

'Let every tongue become a hundred thousand; let each be multiplied twice ten times more. Let this multitude of tongues then join together, each repeating a hundred thousand times the name of creation's Lord.'

(Japji 32)

Some Sikhs stop at the gurdwara on the way to work. Others stop on the way home. They try to keep God in mind all the time. Only very few Sikhs have the Guru Granth Sahib in the home. This is because it must have a room of its own. Most Sikhs have a prayer book which contains hymns from the scriptures.

Discussion question

What would a Sikh family need to discuss before buying a copy of the Guru Granth Sahib to keep at home?

Eating and drinking

Food in the Sikh home varies (**B**). Many Sikhs choose to be vegetarian but they do not have to be. Sikhs must not eat **halal** meat that has been slaughtered in the Muslim way. Alcohol is forbidden. So are all strong **intoxicants** like smoking. Guru Nanak said Sikhs should only be intoxicated by love for God.

Family life

Sikhs are encouraged to marry and have a family. It is through family life that a person learns to love. Men and women may go to

B Sharing food is important in Sikh family life

work. Grandparents may live with the family and help with the children. Children learn the faith from their elders. They must work hard at school as Sikhs believe education is very important.

New words

halal   intoxicants

THINGS TO DO

1 Write down three ways in which the daily life of a Sikh may differ from the daily life of a non-Sikh.

2 Design a poster explaining three teachings or beliefs that guide life in the Sikh home.

3 Is love learnt or does everyone have the ability to love? Discuss this question with a partner. Then write your answer.

4 Sikhs believe we must protect the rights of all people to keep their religious practices and beliefs.
Write down your beliefs about respecting the rights of others.

44 Service to others

Sikhs believe that the soul survives death. It takes on a life in a new body. If a person's actions are good they will be closer to God in the next life. If their actions are evil they will move further away from God. By following the teaching of the Gurus, Sikhs hope to find union with God and be freed from the cycle of rebirth (mukti).

Sewa

All Sikhs try to serve others in their daily lives. Service is called **sewa**. It helps to make the soul pure. It is also an important example to others. Sikhs may help at the gurdwara (**A**). They may visit the sick or raise funds for charity. Sikhs are encouraged to give a tenth of their savings towards the service of the community. This is called **Daswand**.

B Namdhari Sikhs wear homespun cloth as a sign of simplicity, purity and humility

A Sikhs cleaning the pavement outside the Golden Temple, Amritsar

Discussion question

What do you understand by the word 'service'?

Humility and simplicity

Namdhari Sikhs believe simplicity and service are very important. They believe that the line of Gurus continued after Guru Gobind Singh. According to their twelfth Guru, Sikhs must always hide their good deeds from others. Many Namdhari Sikhs wear clothes made from white homespun cloth as a sign of simplicity and humility (**B**). Humility means not putting yourself first.

Sewa means serving those in need no matter who they are.

Bhai Khanaya

Guru Gobind Singh and his men were in battle against the Emperor Aranguzeb. The battle was hard and the Sikhs were tired. In the distance they could see a man giving water to the wounded. It was a Sikh called Bhai Khanaya. He was giving water to the enemy soldiers as well as the Sikhs. The men complained to their Guru that Bhai Khanaya was helping the enemy. Guru Gobind Singh called Bhai Khanaya. 'Is it true?' he asked. 'Yes,' said Bhai Khanaya. 'Many of these men are dying; the least I can do is give them water.' Guru Gobind Singh said that Bhai Khanaya was a true Sikh. All Sikhs must serve the needy, no matter who they are (**C**).

THINGS TO DO

1 Write three sentences on what Sikhs think about service (sewa). Draw a picture to show one way in which a Sikh can serve others.

2 Design a badge or symbol which represents a life of simplicity and humility.

3 Act out the story of Bhai Khanaya in the classroom.

4 Write about an occasion when a person does a good deed but no one knows that they have done it.

New words

sewa   Daswand   Namdhari Sikhs

C Sikhs providing water for thirsty visitors at the Golden Temple, Amritsar

45 Unity and diversity

In each religious tradition there is both **unity** and **diversity**. In other words, the believers share important beliefs but they also do some things differently. For example, all Christians accept Jesus as their Lord and Saviour but they may go to different churches. In some religions the holy book unites people of the same faith. For example, all Jews look to the Torah as the word of God and their guidebook for life (**A**).

Unity and shared practice

The unity of a religion may be

B Salah unites Muslims all over the world

strengthened by things that are done in the same way. For example, salah is the same for all Muslims (**B**). It is sometimes the roots of a religion that gives it its unity. For example, all Hindus look back to India as the place where their faith began. Every religion has something that gives it unity. Something that holds the faith together.

Discussion question

What things do you think hold a religion together?

Diversity in a religion

There are also things that bring about differences, or diversity, in a religion. Sometimes this is in the way people understand the scriptures. For example, the main difference between Orthodox

A The scrolls of the Torah

and Reform Jews is the way they interpret the Torah.

There may be differences in the way people practise their faith. For example, some Hindus worship God at a shrine. Others use yoga and meditation.

The differences within a religion may be due to the climate or culture of where people live. Buddhists in Thailand rely on the community for their daily food (**C**). Buddhists in the UK could not survive in this way.

Serving the needs of different people

Differences in belief and how people worship can sometimes cause conflict. However, shared beliefs can hold the religion together despite the differences. Differences can be a good sign. They show that the needs of different people are being served and that the religion is alive and kicking.

THINGS TO DO

1 Write down three things that hold a faith together in unity. Give an example for each.

2 Choose one religion you have studied. Find three things that unite the people in this religion.

3 Would it be better if all Christians went to the same kind of church? What are the good things about the fact that there are different kinds of churches? Discuss your answer with a partner.

4 Differences in what people believe can cause mistrust and fear. Write a poem or prayer that asks for more trust and understanding between people of different beliefs and faiths.

New words

unity   diversity

C The Buddhist alms round in Thailand

Glossary

A

Abraham first well-known Jewish person. Muslims also respect him as a prophet and a worshipper of Allah

Adhan Muslim call to prayer

Akhirah belief in life after death

Aleinu important Jewish prayer at the end of each service

Allah the Islamic name for God

Alms charity, gift of food

Anglican churches linked to the Church of England

Anicca Buddhist idea that nothing stays the same

Arabic the language of the holy Qur'an

Ardas Sikh formal prayer offered at most religious occasions

Arjuna one of the five Pandava brothers in the Hindu story of the Mahabharata

Ark cupboard in a Jewish synagogue, containing scrolls of the Torah. Also called Aron Hakodesh

Artha to create wealth and material success

Arti Hindu welcoming ceremony involving the offering of light

Atman soul in Hinduism

Avatar the coming down to earth of a deity

B

Baptist branch of the Christian Church

Bhagavad Gita sacred Hindu scriptures

Bhajans religious songs, hymns of praise

Bhakti yoga the way of loving devotion, one of the paths to moksha

Bible name given to the holy scriptures of the Christian faith. Jews sometimes use the name to refer to their scriptures too

Bimah raised platform for reading the Torah in a Jewish synagogue

Bishops high ranking leaders of the Christian Church

Bodhisattva one who puts off becoming a buddha in order to help other living beings

Brahman in Hinduism Universal Spirit, Ultimate Reality, God

Brahmin Hindu priest, priesthood

Buddha enlightened being

C

Canon accepted books of the Bible

Cardinals high ranking leaders of the Roman Catholic Church

Caste system ancient Indian system of dividing people by their job

Chalice cup or goblet used to hold wine in the Christian service of Holy Communion

Challot plural of challah. Bread used on Shabbat and during Jewish festivals

Chauri symbol of authority, a fan waved over the Guru Granth Sahib as a sign of respect

Chazan leader of reading, singing and chanting in synagogue services

Church of England the established Church in England

Creeds statements of religious beliefs

D

Dasam Granth collection of hymns from the tenth of the Sikh Gurus

Daswand one-tenth of a Sikh's savings given to charity

Day of Judgement the last day at the end of time when God will raise the dead and everyone will be judged according to their deeds

Deity god or goddess

Denominations different branches of the Christian Church

Dhamma The truth. The teachings of Gotama Buddha

Dharma Hindu religious duty, law, what is right

Disciples followers or learners taught by a teacher

Diversity variety, with differences

Du'a personal prayer

E

Eightfold Path Gotama Buddha's eight-point guidelines for putting an end to suffering

Elders religious leaders in some Christian denominations

Enlightenment understanding the truth

F

Four Noble Truths Gotama Buddha's teaching which explains why life is as it is

G

Gemara explanations of the Mishnah. Part of the Talmud

Ghee lamp lamp which burns on clarified butter (ghee), used in Hindu worship

Gospels 'good news'. Name given to the books in the Bible which tell about the life of Jesus Christ

Granthi someone who reads the Guru Granth Sahib and leads at Sikh religious ceremonies

Gurbani divine word revealed by the Sikh Gurus

Gurdwara Sikh place of worship

Gurmukhi script of the Punjabi language in which the Guru Granth Sahib is written

Guru spiritual teacher, religious teacher

Guru Granth Sahib Sikh holy scriptures

H

Hadith the sayings of the Prophet Muhammad

Hafiz someone who knows the whole Qur'an by heart

Hajj annual Muslim pilgrimage to Makkah

Halal anything that is permitted under Islamic law

Haram anything that is not permitted under Islamic law

Havdalah Jewish ceremony marking the end of Shabbat

Holy Communion a name given to the service in which Christians share bread and wine

I

Ibadah Muslim acts of faith, e.g. worship, faith in action

Id-ul-Adha Muslim festival of sacrifice

Imam leader, a person who leads prayer at the mosque

Incense substance burnt for its sweet scent, used in worship

Intoxicants alcohol, cigarettes and other drugs not taken for medical purposes

Israel the world-wide community of Jews; the land of Israel; the modern state of Israel

J

Jacob one of the sons of Isaac. Understood to be father of the people of Israel

Jati caste, social group based on what job someone does

Jibril in Islam name for the angel Gabriel

Jnana yoga the way of knowledge, one of the paths to moksha

Jumu'ah Friday prayers at the mosque when a sermon is given

K

Kama sense enjoyment, one of the four aims in life in Hindu tradition

Kamma in Buddhism intentional actions that affect this life and future lives

Karah Parshad blessed food shared out at Sikh worship

Karma in Hinduism deeds, actions, the effects of actions

Karma yoga the way of action, one of the paths to moksh

Ketuvim writings. Part of the Tenakh

Kiddush a Jewish prayer used to make the Shabbat and festival days holy. It is usually recited over wine

Kingdom of God an ideal of Christian life. Some believe it to be a new life Christians have after death. Others think it can be experienced in this life

Kirat Karna in Sikhism earning an honest living by one's own efforts

Kirtan Sikh devotional singing, hymns

Kosher fit, proper. Foods allowed by Jewish food laws

Krishna an avatar or appearance of the God Vishnu. Many Hindus see Krishna as the supreme manifestation of God

Kshatriya warrior and princely class, one of the four classes of traditional Hindu society

L

Langar kitchen where food is prepared at the Sikh gurdwara. Means the community meal

Lay ordinary men and women of a religious community who are not priests or monks or nuns

Lectern stand supporting the Bible

Liberation Theology a Christian movement

Liturgy name given in the Orthodox Church to the service in which bread and wine are shared

M

Mahayana 'great way'. A main form of Buddhism in which belief in bodhisattvas is important

Makkah (sometimes known as Mecca) the Islamic holy city where the Ka'bah is and where Muhammad was born

Mala a string of 108 beads used by Buddhists in prayer or meditation

Mandir Hindu temple containing a shrine to a deity

Manji Sahib stool on which Guru Granth Sahib is placed

Mantra a chant used for worship and meditation

Mass name given to the service in which bread and wine are shared in the Roman Catholic Church

Maya the created world which changes and has no lasting reality

Meditation the control and discipline of the mind which may involve concentration, deep thought and being still

Merit spiritual reward for certain good works and attitudes

Methodists branch of the Christian Church

Metta in Buddhism loving kindness

Mihrab niche in mosque wall indicating direction of Makkah

Minaret tower of a mosque from where call to prayer is given

Ministers religious leaders in some Christian denominations

Minyan ten males over the age of 13, required for a service in many synagogues. Some Jewish communities may include women and others do not even require a minyan for a service

Mishnah first written form of the spoken tradition of Judaism

Moksha in Hinduism freedom from the cycle of karma and samsara, union with God

Monastic order religious group living a life of poverty, chastity and obedience to God

Monks religious men living lives of poverty, chastity and obedience to God

Mosque place of prostration, Muslim place of worship

Mu'adhin one who calls the Islamic faithful to prayer

Muhammad the final prophet sent by Allah to give his message to humankind. Whenever Muslims say his name they add the words 'peace be upon him'. When written this is sometimes shortened to 'pbuh'

Mukti in Sikhism freedom from the cycle of rebirth, union with God

Murtis images used in worship in Hindu temple

N

Namdhari Sikhs Sikhs who base their lives on sinplicity and humility

Nam Simran in Sikhism mediation on the name of God

Ner Tamid the light always burning above the Ark in a synagogue

Nevi'im prophets. Part of the Tenakh

New Testament collection of 27 books which form the second section of the canon of the Christian scriptures

Nibbana 'blowing out'. A state of perfect peace in which greed, hatred and ignorance are no longer felt. Buddhist word for freedom from the bonds of earthly life

Nicene Creed a statement of beliefs recited in many Christian churches

Nuns religious women living lives of poverty, chastity and obedience to God

O

Old Testament part of the canon of Christian scriptures. It has 39 books and was originally written in Hebrew

Orthodox Church branches of the Christian Church traditionally found in Russia, Greece and Eastern Europe

Orthodox Judaism teaches that traditional Jewish practices are important

P

Pali language that buddhist scriptures are wriitten in

Pali Canon the scriptures used by Theravada Buddhists written in the Pali language

Paradise heaven, where the faithful are promised a place after death if they have followed the will of Allah

Passover an important jewish festival celebrated in Spring. It remembers the Exodus from Egypt. Also called Pesach

Pope the head of the Roman Catholic Church, sometimes called the Bishop of Rome

Priests religious leaders

Prophet someone sent by God to speak God's message

Prostrate bow down to the ground in prayer

Puja worship usually involving offerings at a shrine

Q

Qur'an the Muslim holy book, the word of Allah

R

Rabbis ordained Jewish teachers. Often the religious leaders of Jewish communities

Rak'ah a cycle of prayer in Muslim salah

Ramadan Muslim month of fasting

Rebirth being born into a new life

Reform Judaism teaches that Jewish beliefs and practices can be altered to suit changes in people's lifestyles

Risalah Islamic prophethood, channel of communication between Allah and humankind

Roman Catholic Church part of the Christian church led by the Pope

Rupa image of the Buddha

S

Sacraments outward signs of inward blessings

Sadhsangat Sikh congregation of worshippers

Salah Muslim set prayer said five times a day. One of the Five Pillars of Islam

Salvation Army branch of the Christian Church started by William and Catherine Booth

Samsara the Hindu cycle of rebirth

Sangha 'community'. Sometimes the word is used of the community of Buddhist monks (bhikkhus) and nuns (bhikkhunis) and sometimes of the whole Buddhist community

Sawm fasting from dawn to sunset. One of the Five Pillars of Islam

Sefer Torah Torah scroll. The five books of Moses hand-written on parchment and rolled to form a scroll

Shabad hymn in Sikh scriptures

Sewa unselfish service to others

Shabbat Jewish weekly holy day which starts at sunset on Friday and ends at nightfall on Saturday

Shahadah Muslim statement of faith

Shema an important Jewish prayer from the Torah which expresses a clear belief in one God

Shi'ah Muslims who accept Ali as successor after death of the prophet Muhammad

Shirk wrong belief, belief that Allah has an equal or a partner or son

Shrine place where worshippers make offerings, usually containing an image of a god or goddess

Shruti 'revealed', collection of the most ancient and sacred of Hindu scriptures including the Vedas

Shudra servant class, one of the four classes in traditional Hindu society

Simchat Torah Jewish festival when the last part of the Torah is read followed by the first part so the reading starts again for another year

Smriti 'remembered', collection of Hindu scriptures including the Mahabharata and Ramayana

Society of Friends branch of the Christian Church often known as Quakers

Sufi mystic in Muslim tradition which emphasizes the oneness of God and the oneness of all things

Sunni Muslims who accept Abu Bakr as the successor after the death of Muhammad

Surah verse or division of the Qur'an

Synagogue building for Jewish public prayer, study and meeting

T

Takht platform in gurdwara from which the Guru Granth Sahib is read

Tallitot plural of tallit. Four-cornered garment with fringes sometimes worn by Jewish men when they pray

Talmud Mishnah and Gemara collected together

Tawhid belief in the Oneness of Allah

Tenakh the 24 collected books of the Jewish Bible

Ten Sayings Ten rules or sayings from the Torah. Also called the Ten Commandments

Thanka Buddhist painting of buddhas, religious symbols and symbolic scenes

Theravada 'way of the elders'. A main form of Buddhism developed in Sri Lanka and South East Asia

Three Jewels Buddha, Dhamma and Sangha

Tipitaka 'three baskets'. The three parts of the Buddhist Pali scriptures

Torah law or teaching. The five books of Moses

U

Ummah the community of all Muslims

Unity being one

Untouchables a title given to groups in traditional Hindu society who were regarded as outside the four main classes

Upanishads ancient Hindu scriptures belonging to the shruti tradition

V

Vaishya merchant class, one of the four main classes in traditional Hindu society

Vajrayana a form of Buddhism mainly found in Tibet and India

Vand Chhakna sharing what you have with others

Varnas four main classes of traditional Hindu society

Vedas the most ancient and sacred of Hindu scriptures belonging to the shruti tradition

Vicars name given to priests of parishes in the Church of England

Vishnu one of the three main aspects of God in Hinduism

W

Wudu Muslim ritual washing before prayer

Y

Yad hand-held pointer used when reading the Sefer Torah

Yoga discipline of mind, body and life

Z

Zakah giving to the poor and needy, one of the Five Pillars of Islam

feel the presence of God. Sometimes people look at a photo of their family or friends when they want to feel close to them. For many Hindus the murti helps them feel close to God.

B The goddess Durga, her raised hand offers reassurance to the worshipper

The mother goddess (**B**) is known as **Durga** or **Kali** or Parvati. She represents God's power to protect. She carries weapons to overcome the powers of evil. Hindus pray to her to ask for protection from evil.

Symbols work because they draw on feelings as well as thoughts. For example, the pipal tree is a symbol of holiness in India. Its beauty inspires worship and devotion. It represents the link between heaven and earth.

Images in worship

The images used in Hindu worship are called **murtis**. They help the worshipper

---

> **New words**
>
> Brahman Ganesha Durga Kali murtis

THINGS TO DO

1 Write 'What is Brahman?' in a speech bubble coming from the mouth of a person. Give three answers to this question using other people and speech bubbles in your drawing.

2 Look at Photos **A** and **B**. Answer the following questions in full sentences using the photos to help:
   a What can you see that represents the power to fight evil?
   b What do you think represents the beauty of God?
   c What represents the power to remove the things that get in the way of worship?

3 What pictures are important to you? For example, do you keep photos or pictures on your bedroom wall? Draw or describe them and say why they are important to you.

4 A tree is a symbol in many religions. What do you think a tree represents? Design a card which reminds us of all the good things about trees.

5 Symbolic actions and meaning

Symbols are full of meaning. They can be in words or pictures. They can also be actions. For example, sending flowers can mean you want to say thank you. Shaking hands can be a sign of welcome.

Symbolic actions

Symbolic actions play an important part in Hindu worship.

Hindus call worship **puja**. They perform puja at a shrine. A shrine contains an image of a god or goddess.

Performing puja is an expression of love. It includes a number of symbolic actions. For example, the worshipper rings a bell before approaching the image. They wash the image. They also put offerings of food, flowers, light and **incense** before the image.

In this way the worshipper is using the senses of taste, touch, smell, sight and sound to offer love to God.

> 'From the unreal, lead me to the real.
> From darkness lead me to light.
> From death lead me to immortality.'
> (Bhagavad Gita IV, 8)

This is a prayer from the Hindu scriptures. Light is an important symbol. It can stand for the presence of God. It can be a symbol of wisdom and truth. It can also be a sign of life and hope.

Discussion question

Imagine you were lost in the dark and you could see a light in the distance. What would it represent for you?

Light as a sign of welcome

There is a Hindu ceremony call **arti**. It is to welcome God. First the sacred image is washed and offerings of flowers, food and water are given. Then the worshipper lights a lamp. It burns on ghee, or clarified butter. The lamp is raised up and with words of prayer it is waved before the image (**A**).

Then the lamp is taken to the worshippers. They pass their hands across the flame and then over their face and hair

A A Hindu priest turning to perform arti

12

B Worshippers at the temple receiving the arti lamp

(**B**). In this way they receive God's **blessing**.

New words

puja	incense	arti	blessing

THINGS TO DO

1 What symbolic actions are part of everyday life? For example, clapping, waving, bowing? Write down six examples and explain in a sentence what they mean.

2 Describe what is happening in Photo **A**. Say what this ceremony means for Hindus.

3 Put two headings: **a** LIGHT and **b** DARKNESS. Under each write ten words or ideas connected with the heading. For example, under the heading LIGHT, you could put 'Truth' or 'Hope'.

4 How would you show the five senses in a present to someone you love? What objects would you choose as symbols? Draw them and write a sentence on each to explain their meaning.

6 The question of evil in Hinduism

Why is there so much evil in the world? Every religion has a story about how evil came into the world.

The first evil

Hindus believe that ignorance was the first evil. They believe that ignorance can cause suffering. Here is a story which tells how some of the other evils came into the world.

When Brahma had finished creating the world he became hungry. His hunger gave him pains. Out of these came a plague of demons. They attacked him and made him angry. From his anger came all sorts of evils. These wicked spirits set to work bringing evil into the world (**A**).

Discussion question

Is ignorance sometimes the cause of suffering? Can you think of three examples?

The law of karma

Hindus believe in the law of **karma**. Karma means actions. It can also mean what happens as a result of actions. Hindus believe that everything we do has an effect. If we do good we build up good karma. The reward of good karma is a happy life. Selfish or evil actions bring bad karma. If we build up bad karma we suffer for it in the future.

A Out of Brahma's anger came all manner of evils

After death the soul lives on. It is born again in another body. If we have good karma we will be reborn into a good life. If we have bad karma we will be born into a life of suffering.

Lord Krishna

Some of the suffering and evil in the world is too hard for humans to deal with. The Hindu scriptures say that when the forces of evil become too great, the Lord Vishnu comes down to earth. He comes in different forms to help the powers of goodness. He has come as **Rama** and again as Lord **Krishna** to overthrow evil in the world:

'For the protection of the good,
For the destruction of evil-doers...
I come into being age after age.'
(Bhagavad Gita IV, 8)

Many Hindus worship God as Lord Krishna. His birthday is celebrated at the festival of **Janmashtami**. Hindus go to the temple to hear stories about the adventures of Krishna in overcoming evil (**B**). They make offerings at Krishna's shrine. They remember that he saves those who are close to him.

B The young Krishna overcoming Kaliya the serpent who poisoned the waters

New words

karma   Rama   Krishna   Janmashtami

THINGS TO DO

1 Write your own story about how evil came into the world.

2 Sometimes bad things happen to us when we are bad. Can you think of an example of this? Describe how a Hindu person would explain the connection between evil and suffering.

3 In Hindu stories evil comes in different forms. What are the different forms of evil in the world today? Make a poster to illustrate them using newspaper cuttings and pictures.

4 Overcoming evil is an important part of living a good life. Write down two ways in which schools can teach this to children today.

7 Shiva

In some Hindu traditions God is seen as having three faces. These faces represent Brahma, Vishnu and **Shiva**. Brahma is the Creator. Vishnu is the Preserver who comes to earth in different forms to overthrow the powers of evil. Shiva is the Lord of Destruction.

Lord Shiva

One image of Shiva shows him dancing in a circle of flames (**A**). The circle represents the never-ending cycle of life, death and rebirth. The flames symbolize the power to destroy all things. Shiva keeps the rhythm and the heartbeat of the universe by beating the small drum in his hand. Shiva treads on a dwarf which represents ignorance.

Discussion question

When Hindus worship Shiva they are reminded that death is a part of life. Do we remember that death is a part of life or do we try to forget this truth?

Shiva's powers

Shiva not only has the power to destroy all life. He can also make all things new. Sometimes Shiva is represented in a smooth rounded pillar of stone (**B**). This is a symbol of his power to recreate everything.

Perhaps the most well-known image of Shiva is one of him sitting in a **yoga** position in a forest. The Himalayan mountains are in the distance. It is through his deep thought and

A Shiva the Lord of Destruction

B A Hindu worshipping Lord Shiva

meditation that he is able to build up his great powers.

Shivaratri

Many Hindus worship God as Lord Shiva. They keep a night of fasting called Shivaratri. During the fast worshippers gather at the temple for prayer and worship. They make offerings at the shrine and sing hymns of praise.

New words
Shiva   yoga   meditation

THINGS TO DO

1 Design an invitation to the night of fasting at the temple. Write a few sentences to explain the powers of Shiva.

2 Draw Shiva dancing in the circle of flames. Label your picture explaining what the different parts of the image mean.

3 Shiva represents powers of destruction and new life. Write a story in which something old is destroyed and something new is created.

4 Hindus believe that life and death are in God's hands. In your own words try and explain this belief.

8 Pilgrimage in Hinduism

A **pilgrimage** is a journey made for religious reasons. Hindus may go on a pilgrimage to visit a particular shrine or temple. They may go to keep a vow or promise. For example, a childless couple may pray to the goddess Durga for a baby. They may promise to visit her shrine if they have a child.

Sometimes Hindus go on a pilgrimage to prepare for death.

Discussion question

A journey can be a time for learning. Can you think of a journey you have been on where you learnt a lot?

An act of devotion

A pilgrimage is an act of devotion to God. The change of routine is an opportunity to make other changes in life. For example, it may lead to the pilgrim giving more time to prayer and worship. Hindus believe that pilgrimage helps to build up good karma. This may mean they have a better time in the next life.

Pilgrimage involves self-sacrifice, for example, giving up the comforts of home. Many pilgrims save up for years to pay for their journey.

Places of pilgrimage

There are many places of pilgrimage in India. Some Hindus travel to the Himalayan mountains where the holy river Ganges has its source (**A**). Others visit Varanasi. **Varanasi** is on the banks of the river Ganges. Pilgrims gather

A Hindu pilgrims in the Himalayas

B Pilgrims at Varanasi on the banks of the river Ganges

to bathe in the water, to perform puja and to pray (**B**). Hindus believe the waters of the Ganges are so sacred they can wash away bad karma.

Some Hindus go on a pilgrimage to visit a person rather than a place. For example, they may go to hear the teachings of a **guru** or religious teacher.

Hindus in Britain

Hindus in the UK who cannot afford to go to India may go on pilgrimage to Bhaktivedanta Manor. They go to visit

Krishna's shrine there. They may go to the temple in Neasden which is now a sacred place for Hindus in Britain.

New words		
pilgrimage	Varanasi	guru

THINGS TO DO

1 Draw a map of the Indian subcontinent (**C**). Mark a place of pilgrimage on it. Use labels to explain what this place is and what happens there.

2 A change of routine and a change of place can change the way you see things. Write a poem or story which describes the changes taking place on a journey.

3 Choose one place of Hindu pilgrimage,. Draw a scene and write a paragraph about it for a Hindu travel brochure.

4 If you were to make a pilgrimage where would you go? Explain your choice.

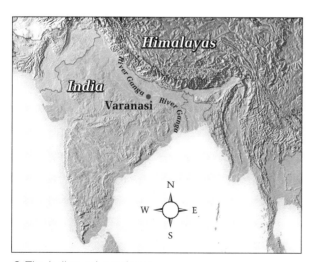

C The Indian subcontinent

9

Judaism: the Covenant

Judaism is a very old religion. **Jews** believe in one God.

The Covenant with Abraham

Jews believe God wanted people to know and love him. About 2000 BCE a man called **Abraham** wanted to know God. God spoke to him. They made an agreement. Abraham promised to do anything God wanted. Abraham proved he would. One day God asked him to **sacrifice** his son, Isaac. He got ready to kill Isaac. Just then God stopped him. He gave him a ram to sacrifice instead.

God rewarded Abraham for keeping his promise. He said he would make him the father of a great nation. They would have the land of **Canaan** to live in. This promise was called the **Covenant**.

Abraham's Family

Abraham had a son called Isaac. Isaac had a son called Jacob. Jacob's name was changed to Israel. He had twelve sons. From their families grew the twelve tribes of Israel (**A**).

Discussion question

Do you know the names of all your relatives who are alive? Do you know the names of older relatives who have died? Are you interested in the history of your family?

A Windows showing the twelve tribes of Israel. They are in the Hadassah Medical Centre in Jerusalem

B A Torah scroll

The Covenant with Moses

Abraham's family became a nation. It needed a new Covenant. The people had lived as slaves in Egypt. **Moses** had helped them escape. He led them back to the land God had promised them. Jews believe God spoke with Moses on Mount Sinai (see Unit 13). He gave the Jews guidelines for life.

The Torah

God's promises and commandments were written down in the **Torah** (**B**). It was a sign of the special agreement between God and Israel. It reminded the people that they should love God and keep his commandments. In return, God promised to protect and care for them. They would live in the land God promised them. This later became known as Israel.

Judaism in Britain

The first Jews arrived in Britain in the eleventh century. They were treated badly and sent away. In 1655 CE Jews were allowed to live in Britain again. In the nineteenth century Jews escaped to Britain to avoid persecution (**C**).

C A nineteenth-century synagogue in Manchester. It is now used as a museum

New words

Jews   Abraham   sacrifice   Canaan
Covenant   Moses   Torah
Ten Commandments

THINGS TO DO

1 Sacrifice always means giving up something which is difficult. Sometimes people sacrifice their time or their freedom. Make a list of examples of people giving up their time or their freedom. Think particularly of yourself and people who look after you and teach you. You may be able to think of examples from the news as well.

2 In the Torah there are guidelines for life. Perhaps the most famous are the Ten Sayings or **Ten Commandments.** Three of these are:
• Keep the Sabbath day holy
• Respect your father and your mother
• Do not desire what belongs to others.
Look at each of these sayings in turn. Think of at least one way in which each might be helpful today.

3 During our lives we make lots of agreements with all sorts of people. Make a poster to show the two sides of agreements between
• parents and children
• teachers and students

4 This unit talks about times when jews have been badly treated by others. Find out and explain what the words religious intolerence mean. Can you think of or find out about examples of religious intolerence?

10

Symbols in Judaism

Jews of today still obey God's commandments.

The mezuzah

The Torah tells Jews to write the commandments on the doorposts of their houses. A symbol of this is a **mezuzah** (**A**). It is found on doorposts of Jewish homes. It is a scroll in a small container. A section of the Torah is written in Hebrew.

The words are from a prayer called the **Shema**. It begins, 'Hear O Israel, the Lord our God is One…'. Many Jews touch the mezuzah as they pass through the door. This reminds them of God's love.

Discussion question

Is there anything you think you should remember every day? Why?

A A mezuzah on a doorpost in a Jewish home

B Some Jewish men wear the tefillin and tallit as a sign of the Covenant with God

Tefillin

The Torah also says Jews should tie the commandments on their arms and wear them on their foreheads. On weekdays many Jewish men wear **tefillin** when they pray. These are two small leather boxes. Inside are pieces of parchment with parts of the Torah on them. One box is strapped on the forehead. The other is tied to the weaker arm.

Tallit

Many Jewish men also wear a **tallit** when they pray (**B**). This is a rectangle of fabric with tassels on the corners. This is because the Torah tells them to make tassels on the corners of their clothes. Some Jewish men wear an undervest with tassels on. This is called a **tzizit**. The tassels are a reminder of the commandments (**C**).

Food laws

There are rules about food in the Torah. Jews may only eat foods which are 'fit'. The word for this is **kosher**. For example, fish must have both fins and scales. Meat must come from animals which chew the cud and have parted hooves. All meat must have the blood drained

from it. Animals should be killed in a special way. There are Jewish butchers who make sure that meat is dealt with in the correct ways.

Meat and milk products may not be eaten in the same meal. In some homes there might be different plates and pots for meat and milk. Some homes have two sinks. One is for washing up after meat foods. The other is for washing up after milk foods.

Following these rules helps remind Jews of God all through each day.

C Jewish boys wearing tzizit to remind them to keep God's commands

---

New words

mezuzah   Shema   tefillin   tallit
tzizit   kosher

THINGS TO DO

1 Keeping the commandments of the Torah helps Jews to be part of their community. What are the symbols, customs and rules which make your school a community?

2 Some Jews try to keep all the commandments. Some people think some of them are out of date.
What are the good things about:
• religious traditions staying the same
• religious traditions changing through time?
Discuss these questions in class.

3 Plan the meals for a Jewish family for one day. Think carefully about what meats and fish may be eaten. Remember not to use meat and milk in the same meal.

4 Jewish parents must teach the commandments to their children. Make a poster to show what you have learnt about kosher food laws.

11

Creation

Jews believe God created the world and that he cares for it. The story of how the world was created is in the Torah.

In the beginning there was nothing. First God made day and night (**A** and **B**). On the second day God made water into oceans and rain. Dry land and plants were

A & B God created night and day

made on the third day. Next God made the sun to light the day and the moon to light the night. Creatures of the oceans and the air were made on the fifth day. God made all the animals of the earth on the sixth day. Then he said, 'Let me make a human. Someone like me, to rule over the other creatures.' So he created man and woman.

God blessed the man and the woman. He said they should have children. They should also look after the other creatures in the world. He was pleased with what he had made.

Discussion question

Jews and Christians believe human beings were made to be like God. In what ways do you think humans might be like God?

On the seventh day God rested. He made it a holy day.

Understanding the story

Some Jews believe this story describes exactly what happened. Others do not. However, most agree that it has meaning for people today. It shows that God is powerful and he cares for the world. Some people say the word 'day' might stand for a very long time. This could mean the story is about the world developing over millions of years.

The story suggests that human beings are God's most important creation. They have the job of caring for everything else (**C**).

C Humans are supposed to look after the animals. These lion skins are for sale as rugs.

D Trees are planted during Tu B'Shevat celebrations

One way Jews care for God's world is the festival of Tu B'Shevat where they plant trees (**D**).

New words

Shabbat

THINGS TO DO

1 Work in groups to prepare a short radio programme. It will be a group of people talking about different ways of understanding the story of creation. One person in the group will be the interviewer. Each of the others will pick one way of understanding the story. They will take it in turns to explain what they believe the story teaches.

2 The story of creation shows God gave human beings power over nature. It is also their job to look after everything else in the world. Make a poster to show how you and your friends could look after your school and the area around it.

3 Jews believe God gave human beings the job of caring for animals and the world around them. Some people say they have not done this job very well (**C**). Collect some information and pictures to show how people have:
• been cruel to animals
• not carefully looked after the world
• tried to care for animals and the world around them.

4 In the creation story God rested on the seventh day. Jews follow this example. They keep the seventh day as a day of rest. It is called **Shabbat**. Do you think that one day each week should be different from the rest? In what way should it be different?

12

Rosh Hashanah and Yom Kippur

T he most holy days of the Jewish year are **Rosh Hashanah** (New Year) and **Yom Kippur** (the Day of Atonement). They happen in autumn.

Rosh Hashanah

At the New Year Jews think about the past year. They try to put right their mistakes and make a fresh start. They ask for God to forgive them. They also ask to be forgiven by people they have hurt or upset. In return, people then have a duty to forgive those who ask for forgiveness.

Discussion question

It is not always easy to forgive other people. What sorts of things would you find most difficult to forgive? Why?

At New Year Jews wear new clothes. They eat fruits that have just come into season. Pieces of apple are dipped in honey (**A**). This shows that people hope the new year will be a sweet one.

In **synagogues** a ram's horn is blown one hundred times. It is called a **shofar** (**B**). The sound surprises people. It reminds them to repent. This means to say sorry for the things they have done wrong.

A Apples are dipped in honey to show hope for the new year ahead

B The shofar being blown at Rosh Hashanah

Yom Kippur

The Day of Atonement comes ten days after Rosh Hashanah. Atone means 'at one'. To live at one with God means to repent and obey the commandments. Jews listen to the story of how Abraham obeyed God when he nearly sacrificed his son Isaac (see Unit 9).

Yom Kippur is a day of fasting, praying and listening to the Torah. Lots of people go to synagogues. In the afternoon the book of Jonah is read. The story shows God will forgive anyone who is really sorry (see box).

Jews believe God looks in the book of life. At Yom Kippur he decides if a person's name should stay in the book or if they should die. The day ends with one note from the shofar. It reminds Jews to keep the Covenant and live 'at one' with God.

New words

Rosh Hashanah   Yom Kippur
synagogue   shofar

The story of Jonah

God told Jonah to go to the city of Nineveh. People there were behaving badly. Jonah was to tell them God was angry. Jonah did not want to do this so he got on a ship going somewhere else. Soon a storm blew up. Jonah thought God had sent the storm to punish him. He told the sailors to throw him into the sea. The storm stopped. A big fish swallowed Jonah. He prayed.

After three days the fish spewed him on to a beach. He went to Nineveh. He told the people God would punish them for their wickedness. They listened to him. They dressed in sackcloth and fasted to show how sorry they were. God saw that they were truly sorry and so he did not punish them. Jonah was cross that God had changed his mind. God showed him that it would not be fair to punish people who were truly sorry.

THINGS TO DO

1 Make a list of things Jews do at Rosh Hashanah. Make another list of things they do at Yom Kippur. Which of these things interests you most? Why?

2 Read the story of Jonah in the box. Many people believe this teaches some important lessons. Answer these questions:
   a How did Jonah find out he should have obeyed God?
   b How did Jonah know what God wanted him to do?
   c Why did God forgive the people of Nineveh?
   d How does the story show God has power?
   e Why do people today try to do what they think God wants?

3 Rosh Hashanah is a time of judgement. God decides whether people should be punished. If people believe God will punish them for what they do wrong do you think it will make a difference to the way they live? Discuss your ideas with your class.

4 A fresh start usually means people setting targets for being better. Write down and explain the targets you would set yourself for the next year.

13 God's care for his people

Jews believe their ancestors were slaves in Egypt. The Pharaoh of Egypt would not let them go. Jews believe God chose a man called Moses to help them escape. Then ten disasters happened. They are usually called the ten plagues. The last one was the death of the eldest son in every Egyptian family. Children of the slaves did not die because Moses told them how to be safe. They had to kill lambs and put the blood on the doorposts of their homes. God's angel of death passed over and did not visit these families.

The Pharaoh told the slaves to leave Egypt straight away. They did not even have time to put yeast in their bread dough so it would rise.

Jews believe God helped Moses to lead the people as they travelled in the desert. They had to build shelters because they were homeless. They relied on God to protect them. At Mount Sinai Jews believe God gave Moses the Torah. This gave people guidelines to live by.

Remembering God's care

There are three festivals which remind Jews of these difficult times and how God helped their ancestors.

Pesach
The festival of **Pesach** is a reminder of the escape from Egypt.

Sukkot
The festival of **Sukkot** reminds Jews of how God protected their ancestors when they were living in shelters in the desert. Jewish families build shelters called sukkot (**A**). They eat their meals in them

A A sukkah reminds Jews of how God protected their ancestors in the desert.

B The lulav and etrog are symbols used at Sukkot

during the festival. Many people also sleep in them. The roofs are made of branches and leaves. They are not weatherproof.

Jews remember that God cares for the whole world. As a symbol of this they wave a lulav and etrog (**B**). The etrog is a fruit like a lemon. The lulav is made from branches of three plants. Some say these four things stand for different parts of the body. These parts are: the heart, spine, lips and eyes. They remind Jews that they should use their whole bodies to do God's work.

At **Shavuot** Jews remember the time when God gave Moses the Torah (**C**).

Discussion question

How do you think people could use their hearts, spines, lips and eyes to do God's work?

New words

Pesach   Sukkot   Shavuot

C The ten commandments (part of the Torah) on tablets of stone in a synagogue

THINGS TO DO

1 Every year Jews remember the escape of the slaves from Egypt. Imagine you were one of those slaves. Write or act out the story of your last few days in Egypt and how you escaped.

2 Look in the first section of this unit. Can you work out why the English name for Pesach is Passover? Explain the reasons in your own words.

3 Shavuot and Sukkot are both harvest festivals. Harvest usually makes people think about how we get our food. It could be about how we get other things. The harvest of hard work at school might be passing exams. Plan a harvest celebration which is not about food. It must be about giving thanks for other things we need in life today.
   a What might people want to say thank-you for at this celebration?
   b Write a thank-you prayer which everyone could read at this celebration.
   c What pictures could you choose to go on the walls?

Pesach

At the festival of Pesach there is a special service called the **seder**. It includes a meal and starts with the lighting of candles.

The Hagadah

The youngest child asks, 'Why is this night different from all other nights?' The leader of the seder answers. He tells the story of the slaves escaping from Egypt.
Everyone can follow the story in a book called the **Hagadah**.

Special foods

The seder includes a meal. There are special foods on the table to remind people of parts of the story (**A**).

- Matzah is bread without yeast. It reminds Jews of how quickly the slaves had to leave Egypt. They did not have time to let their bread dough rise.

- A lamb bone is a reminder of the lambs which were killed. The blood was put on the doorposts of homes to protect them from God's angel of death.

- A roasted egg is a symbol of sacrifices made in the temple.

- Maror is bitter herbs. This can be lettuce or horseradish. They remind Jews of how horrible slavery was.

- Haroset is a mixture of apples, cinnamon, nuts and wine. It stands for the cement used by the slaves in building work.

- Carpas is a sign of spring. It is a green vegetable, often parsley. It is dipped in salt water to remind people of the slaves' tears.

Wine

Everyone has wine during the seder meal. A glass is also poured out for the **prophet Elijah**. Jews believe he will come again before all the people of the world are free. Someone may open the door to see if he has arrived. In Britain in the twelfth century some people said Jews drank blood at Pesach. When they opened the door it showed this was not true.

A The symbolic foods of the seder meal

Discussion question

Why do you think people sometimes say untrue things about other people's religions? Can you suggest ways of preventing this?

B Candles are lit each night of Hanukkah

Hanukkah

Hanukkah is another festival when Jews remember an escape from persecution. At Hanukkah Jews celebrate how the Maccabees got control of the temple from the Greeks who had captured it. They light candles or oil lamps every night of the festival. It lasts for eight days (**B**).

Purim

Purim is fun (**C**). The serious side of it is remembering how Jews escaped from the Persian Empire.

C There are often fancy dress parades and parties to celebrate Purim

THINGS TO DO

1 A local primary school has found out that your class is studying Pesach. You have been asked to set up a display about the seder meal at the primary school. It should show the young children about this part of Pesach. Work in a group. Decide what you will put in your display. What writing will you put on your display to help explain it?

2 Some strict families will use different pots, plates and cutlery during Pesach. This is so they have not touched leavened foods. Leaven is anything which will make dough rise. It could be yeast or self-raising flour. If you did not want to use things which had touched leavened food, you would have to have different cooking and eating equipment for Pesach. Make a list of all the things you would need.

3 Light is an important symbol used at Hanukkah. Food is an important part of Pesach.
   a Make two lists: one about lights and the other about foods. Write down ways they are used in celebrations you know about.
   b Choose either light or food. See if you can find out more about how it is used in Jewish festivals.

4 The stories of Pesach, Hanukkah and Purim tell of how Jewish people helped to rescue their communities. The United Nations Declaration of Human Rights says that everyone has duties to the community. What do you think are your duties to:
   • your school community,
   • the community you live in?

New words

seder   Hagadah   prophet   Elijah   Hanukkah   Purim

15

Israel

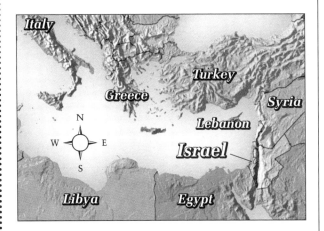

A Map showing the position of Israel

Jews live all over the world. For many of them Israel is a very special place (**A**). They believe God promised this land to Abraham when he made the Covenant. Many Jews want to visit Israel. It is a chance to feel in touch with the traditions and history of their people and religion.

Jerusalem

There are many interesting places in Israel. Perhaps the most important place in Israel is the holy city of **Jerusalem**. There used to be a temple there. It was first built in the tenth century BCE. It was destroyed and rebuilt. It was the centre of Jewish worship for hundreds of years. The temple was the only place where sacrifices could be made. People used to travel there to celebrate festivals, especially Pesach, Sukkot and Shavuot.

Discussion question

What does the word 'sacrifice' mean to you today?

The Western Wall

The temple was finally destroyed in 70 CE. All that remains today is part of the outer wall. This is known as the Western Wall (**B**). Many Jews like to visit it because it reminds them of their history. It links

B Worshippers at the Western Wall in Jerusalem

C Yad Vashem is a memorial to those who died in the Holocaust

D A light is kept burning in the hall of remembrance at Yad Vashem

them with people throughout the years who have worshipped there.

Many Jews go to the Western Wall to pray. Some like to write their prayers on small pieces of paper and put them in between the great stones. The area is always very crowded on Shabbat and at festival times.

Yad Vashem

Another place in Israel which many people visit is called Yad Vashem (**C**). It is a memorial to Jews who died in the **Holocaust**. The **Gentiles** who helped them are also remembered here. A light is kept burning in the large hall of remembrance (**D**). On the floor are the names of camps in which Jews died. Visitors are reminded of just how many died. Six million Jews lost their lives.

The Western Wall and Yad Vashem are two places which remind Jews of their history.

New words

Jerusalem   Holocaust   Gentiles

THINGS TO DO

1 Make a list of reasons why Israel is a special place for Jews. Unit 9 on pages 20 – 21 will help you as well.

2 The Temple in Jerusalem was the centre of Jewish worship for hundreds of years. Jews still go to worship at the remains today. Do you think it is important for people to have special buildings where they can worship God? Or can people worship God anywhere? Talk about this in your class. Make a list of advantages of having places of worship. Can you think of anything to put in a list of disadvantages?

3 Some people try to say the Holocaust did not happen. Others think it is very important to teach young people about it. Think of as many reasons as you can:
   • why it might be a good idea to teach young people today about the Holocaust
   • why so many Jews and non-Jews visit Yad Vashem.
   Do you think there are any good reasons for trying to forget the Holocaust?

4 Look carefully at pictures **C** and **D**. Try to explain how they make you feel.

16

The spread of Buddhism

Gotama Buddha

Buddhism began with Gotama **Buddha** in northern India. He was born in about 563 BCE. Buddha means enlightened being. This is someone who understands the truth about life. Then he taught others how to find **enlightenment**. His teachings became popular. He had many followers. They came to be known as **Buddhists**.

The Buddha's followers spread his message after he had passed away. They went to other parts of India. They took Buddhism south-east to Sri Lanka, Myanmar and Thailand. They went north-east to Nepal, Bhutan, China and Japan (**A**).

Emperor Asoka

Emperor Asoka ruled most of India in the third century BCE. Many battles had been fought to make his empire bigger. He was sad to find out how many people had died in these battles. He listened to Buddhist teachers and became a Buddhist himself.

After this he worked hard to build a peaceful society. He sent out **missionaries** to spread the Buddha's teachings. Asoka believed it was important for people to respect other's religions.

Discussion question

Why do you think Asoka wanted more and more people to hear about the Buddha's teachings?

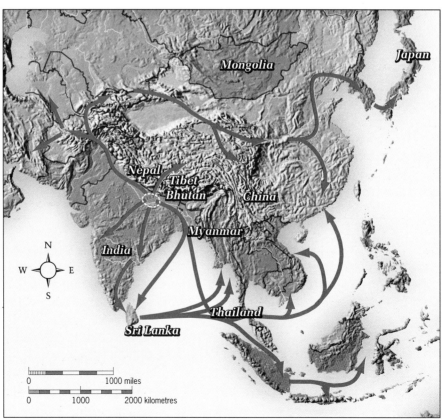

A After the Buddha passed away, his followers travelled to spread his teachings.

B Monks travelled to Britain to teach about Buddhism

C Western Buddhists at Chithurst monastry in the south of England

Different forms of Buddhism

Over the years three main types of Buddhism could be seen. In Sri Lanka, Myanmar and Thailand **Theravada** Buddhism is the main form of the religion. Theravada Buddhists scriptures are called the **Pali Canon**. **Mahayana** Buddhism is the strongest form of Buddhism in China and Japan. In Tibet and Mongolia it is **Vajrayana** Buddhism. The different forms of Buddhism teach slightly different ways to enlightenment.

Buddhism in the West

People in Europe and the USA did not really know much about Buddhism until the nineteenth century. Buddhism was not practised in Britain until the twentieth century. In 1926 the Buddhist Society was formed. Buddhists travelled to Britain from other countries to teach about Buddhism (**B**). Buddhists from a number of countries settled in Britain.

However, most Buddhists in Britain are people who have personally chosen to follow this way of life (**C**).

New words

Buddha   enlightenment   Buddhists
missionaries   Theravada   Pali canon
Mahayana   Vajrayana

THINGS TO DO

1   Draw a map to show countries where Buddhism is one of the main religions. Use three different colours to show the areas where Theravada, Mahayana and Vajrayana Buddhism grew up.

2   Emperor Asoka thought it was important that people should respect one another's religious beliefs. Young people in Britain have to study Religious Education. They learn about the worldís great religions. Do you think this might help them to respect one another's religious beliefs? Try to explain the reasons for your answer.

3   Can you think up five pieces of advice which might help people in the world to live more peacefully together? Would this advice be helpful to your school community? If yes, explain how.

4   Missionaries travelled to tell people about the Buddha's teachings. Buddhism spread into many different countries. People in different countries followed the teachings of the Buddha in different ways. Why do you think these

17

Gotama Buddha

All forms of Buddhism are based on the life and teaching of Gotama Buddha. He was a prince in northern India. He was called Siddhattha Gotama.

Siddhattha's birth

Siddhattha's mother had a strange dream before he was born. She dreamt that a white elephant entered her side. White elephants are very rare. She felt this was a sign that the child would be unusual.

A wise man said the boy would grow up to be a great and powerful ruler. However, if he saw any suffering he would become a wise holy man.

Siddhattha grows up

Siddhattha's father did not want his son to give up everything and become a holy man. He made sure the boy never heard or saw any suffering.

When Siddhattha was a young man he got married. He had a child of his own. However, he felt restless. One day he asked his driver to take him outside the palace. The things he saw outside changed his life. He saw an old person (**A**). He saw a sick person in pain. He saw a dead body ready to be **cremated**. Then he saw a holy man who had given up everything he owned (**B**). This man had a special look about him.

A Gotama saw old age for the first time

B Gotama saw a holy man and gave up all he owned

Siddhattha joined a group of holy men in the forest. They had given up everything to search for the truth about life. He tried the hardest **meditation** exercises.

Discussion question

Siddhattha Gotama saw four things which changed his life. Have you ever seen anything which has had a strong effect on you? It could be something pleasant or upsetting.

He fasted (went without food) until he nearly died. None of this worked.
He began to eat again. His friends left him in disgust. He sat under a **Bodhi tree** (**C**) to meditate. He made up his mind not to move until he understood the truth about life.

Enlightenment

Siddhattha gained enlightenment under the Bodhi tree. he found **Nibbana**.
Nibbana means 'blown out' like a flame. Some people say it is like being set free.

New words

cremated   meditation   Bodhi tree
Nibbana

C The Bodhi tree, also known as the Tree of Wisdom

THINGS TO DO

1 Siddhattha Gotama's father made sure he did not see signs of suffering. Parents like to protect their children from sadness and suffering. Discuss whether you think this is a good idea? Would you like your parents to do this for you? How could you try to do this for your children?

2 When Siddhattha went outside the palace for the first time he saw three things which shocked him. Explain in your own words why each of these things had such a strong effect on him. He also saw a holy man. How did this help to change his life?

3 Plan a book for very young children about the life of the Buddha. This book should have a picture and writing on each page. It must have six pages. Work out what should go on each one.

4 How important do you think money is in making people happy? Make a collage showing things that give you real happiness.

18

Buddha images

For Buddhists Gotama Buddha was a very special man. He achieved enlightenment.

Homes and **shrine** rooms usually have images of the Buddha. These are looked after very carefully. They remind Buddhists of the Buddha and his teaching. Offerings of flowers, **incense** and light are made as a sign of respect.

Positions

Images of the Buddha are called **rupas**. There are different kinds. The most well known show the Buddha sitting. Others show him standing or lying down.

Muddas

Rupas have different hand gestures. They are called **muddas**. Each one means something different. One hand resting on the other is a symbol of meditation (**A**). Fingers making a circle show the Buddha teaching. The right hand pointing down and turned outwards is a sign of giving. The right hand raised with the palm turned outwards means blessing (**B**).

A Buddha in meditation

B Buddha offering protection and blessing

It gives a feeling of protection. A seated Buddha with his right hand touching the ground reminds people of the Buddha meditating before his enlightenment (**C**). While he was meditating the god of death sent many things to distract him. He did not give in to the things that tempted him.

He touched the earth so that it could see he had not been tempted or distracted.

Discussion question

What distracts you when you are trying to concentrate? What helps you to concentrate?

Other features

Long earlobes are a reminder of the heavy jewellery he wore when he lived in the palace.

There is usually a bump on his head. It is a reminder of the kind of headwear he wore as a prince. It probably looked like a turban. Some people say this bump is a sign of his wisdom. On some rupas it is long and pointed. It can also be shaped like flames. It is a symbol of enlightenment. On some rupas it is the hood of a snake. This reminds people of a story. In it a snake called Mucalinda protected the Buddha from a storm while he was meditating.

New words

shrine   incense   rupas   muddas

THINGS TO DO

1 Many people say that images of the Buddha make them feel at peace.

C Gotama Buddha meditating before enlightenment

Look at the photos in this unit and try to say how they make you feel.

2 Make a poster to explain what different Buddha rupas mean. Think of the different muddas they might have. Also include other features which show the Buddha was a special person.

3 Buddha rupas are always treated with great care and respect. How do you think Buddhists show their care and respect for a Buddha rupa? Look carefully at the pictures in this unit to help you.

4 Gestures are powerful ways of giving messages. Work in a group. List as many hand gestures as you can think of and explain what they mean. These meanings might be friendly or unfriendly.

19

Symbols in Buddhism

In Buddhism different symbols are used.

Symbols of enlightenment

The Bodhi tree is a symbol of enlightenment. Siddhattha gained enlightenment under one of these trees. The lotus flower is also a symbol of enlightenment. It grows out of deep muddy water. It becomes a most beautiful flower. Images of the Buddha are often seated on a lotus flower.

The wheel

The wheel is a very old Indian symbol. In Buddhism it is drawn with eight spokes. This is a symbol of the **Eightfold Path** (**A**). These are the guidelines for life which Gotama Buddha taught.

Other Buddhas

Another image of Buddhism is often called the Laughing Buddha (**C**). This is not Gotama Buddha. It is a Buddha who will come in the future. He looks well fed and happy. This shows what life will be like when he comes.

Avalokiteshvara

In Mahayana Buddhism there is a strong belief in **bodhisattvas**. A bodhisattva is someone who puts off Nibbana to help others gain enlightenment. One of the most well known is **Bodhisattva Avalokiteshvara** (**B**). He has never-ending

A The Buddhist wheel with eight spokes

B Bodhisattva Avalokiteshvara

C The Laughing Buddha

kindness and feeling for other people. He sees how people struggle with life. He wants to help everyone towards happiness. For this reason he has eleven heads and a thousand arms. In each hand he holds something with which to help others. On each hand there is an eye. This helps him to see the true needs of people. There are objects in the hands to enable him to help others.

Discussion question

Always being kind to others can be quite difficult. What are the rewards of being kind and helpful to others? Why is it difficult?

The Three Jewels

The western Buddhist Order uses a badge of the **Three Jewels**. The jewels are the Buddha, the **Dhamma** and the **Sangha**.

New words

Eightfold Path   bodhisattvas
Bodhisattva Avalokiteshvara
Three Jewels   Dhamma   Sangha

D The Three Jewels

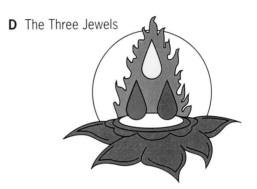

THINGS TO DO

1 If you wanted to help other people like Bodhisattva Avalokiteshvara, what objects would you choose to help you with the job? Explain why you would choose these things.

2 Draw a table with two columns. In one column name or draw all the symbols of Buddhism mentioned in this chapter. In the other column explain what each one means.

3 The Sangha helps people find greater understanding and enlightenment. How can being part of a religious community strengthen a person's faith? You might like to think about other religions you have studied as well to help you answer this question.

4 Many clubs and groups have rules or guidelines for members to follow. Find out whether any people in your class belong to such groups. Write a report of your findings. It should say what the good and bad things are about being members.

20

Important occasions

There are a number of special days each year for Buddhists.

Rains retreat

The first Buddhist **monks** could not travel during the rainy season to spread the Buddha's teachings. It was too difficult to get around. At this time each year they had to take shelter. This became known as the **Rains retreat**. Nowadays even where there is no rainy season, monks stay in their own **temple** at this time.

Lay Buddhists visit them with gifts of food. These are people who are not monks or nuns.

Some lay Buddhists try to pay more attention to their religion at this time. They might stay at a **monastery** for a while. In this way the Sangha and lay people support one another. Lay people bring gifts of food. The Sangha gives them spiritual guidance. In some places the Shangha also provides education for boys and young men (sometimes girls as well) (**A**).

Kathina ceremony

At the end of the Rains Retreat there is an important ceremony. It is called the **Kathina** ceremony. Kathina means cloth or robe. Lay people give the Sangha cloth to make a new robe (**B**). It has to be cut out and made by the monks. It must be finished in one day. Buddhists gain **merit**, or spiritual reward, by giving the cloth. This means it will help them towards a better rebirth, or next life.

Discussion question

Why do you think Buddhist monks often wear robes like those in Photo **B** instead of the ordinary clothes of their region?

A Boys are educated by some Sanghas

B Lay Buddhists give bhikkhus (monks) cloth at

Uposatha days

Theravada Buddhists have **Uposatha** days every month. **Bhikkus** (monks) and **bhikkhunis** (nuns) think and speak about their mistakes and weaknesses. This helps them improve. Many Buddhists go to shrines and listen to Buddhist teachings.

The Western Buddhist Order

The Western Buddhist Order has three special days. They are days of celebration and meditation. On Buddha Day people celebrate the enlightenment of the Buddha. They remember his wisdom and kindness. Dhamma Day is about the Buddha's teaching and how it can spread (**C**). The theme of Sangha Day is friendship and harmony.

C Balloons released at Dhamma Day celebrations

New words
monks   Rains Retreat   temple Lay   monastery   Kathina   merit Uposatha   Bhikkus   bhikkhunis

THINGS TO DO

1 In the rainy season Buddhists monks stay in their monasteries. Imagine you were staying out in the country for one month with no television or other entertainment. Discuss how you could make this time valuable.

2 The Sangha and lay people in Buddhism support one another. The Sangha gives lay people 'spiritual guidance'. What do you think this might mean? Can you think of other groups which support one another? How do they do this?

3 Why do you think Buddhist monks and nuns are asked to think and speak about their mistakes and weaknesses? How might this help them to improve? How do you think you would feel if you were asked to do this?

4 Peace and harmony are important in Buddhism. Design a symbol or make a collage to show these ideas.

21 Festivals of the Buddha

Wesak is the most well-known Buddhist festival. People show their respect for the Buddha and his teachings.

Discussion question

What does it mean to show respect for something or someone?

Wesak celebrations

There are many ways to celebrate Wesak. In some places lanterns are lit around temples and shrines. Temples may have a Bodhi tree. This is a symbol of the Buddha's enlightenment. At Wesak the tree is watered and decorated with lanterns. Lay Buddhists take gifts of food for monks. Offerings are put in front of the Buddha rupa. Lights stand for the understanding that the Buddha's teaching can bring. They are also symbols of his enlightenment. Flowers show how fragile and short life is (**A**). People change and die. When the Buddha was enlightened he came to understand that nothing can stay the same forever.

People listen to talks about the Dhamma (**B**). In Buddhist countries these talks might be on radio and television so people can hear them at home. Some lay Buddhists spend this special time fasting. Some will be silent. In this way they remember the passing away of the Buddha as well as his enlightenment.

There are Wesak parties for children. Many adults practise meditation. Some go and live with the Sangha for the festival.

A Flowers are offered to show how fragile and short life is

B Buddhists listen to talks about the Dhamma

C The Esala Perahera. The elephant is carrying a copy of the container in which the Buddha's tooth is said to be kept

Esala Perahera

Some festivals have become famous even though they are not celebrated by all Buddhists. One of these is celebrated in Kandy, in Sri Lanka. Buddhists believe that one of the Buddha's teeth is in a temple there. The **Esala Perahera** takes place in July/August. Every evening for two weeks there are great processions through the streets.

On the last night an elephant carries a copy of the container which holds the Buddha's tooth. The actual container with the tooth is too valuable to go out in the street. There is great excitement as people crowd the pavements. The music is loud. The torches of flame make it hot. The elephants wear colourful covers and have lights around their bodies. They look spectacular (**C**).

The Buddha's tooth is a treasured **relic**. This festival shows how special people think it is.

New words

Wesak   Esala Perahera   relic

THINGS TO DO

1 Make a leaflet for a Buddhist temple in Britain. It is to advertise Wesak. It should explain what the festival is about. It should also invite people to join in the celebrations.

2 Some Buddhists spend part of the Wesak festival in silence. Discuss how you feel about being silent. You may feel different about silence in different situations. Think about how you feel at these different times. Try to explain your feelings.

3 Why do you think some Buddhists remember the Buddha's passing away by fasting and being silent?

4 The Esala Perahera is a great tourist attraction. So is the temple in Kandy. When local people go there to worship, there are often many tourists watching what is going on. They are not there to worship. Make a list of the advantages and disadvantages of letting tourists in to the temple at times of worship.

22

Pilgrimage

Gotama Buddha said his followers should visit four places which were important in his life. These were the places of his birth, enlightenment, first sermon and passing away.

Bodh Gaya

Many pilgrims go to Bodh Gaya each year. This is where Gotama sat under the Bodhi tree until he gained enlightenment (**A**). The temple there has a statue of Gotama Buddha. Near the temple is a Bodhi tree.

A The Temple at Bodh Gaya

Pilgrims tie prayer flags to the Bodhi tree nearby. They sit and meditate underneath it. There is also a special stone there. People say it has the Buddha's footprint on it. This is a symbol of his presence.

Stupas

There are also special places for Buddhists to visit outside India. After the Buddha passed away, some of his remains were buried in mounds in different places. These remains were called relics. They might be teeth, pieces of hair or even some of the Buddha's ashes.

The relics were put in **stupas**. These are burial mounds. Stupas became places of pilgrimage (**B**).

Discussion question

In many religions it is common to have memorials to mark lives. Why do you think they are important?

B A stupa

Sri Pada

Another popular place to visit is Sri Pada in Sri Lanka (**C**). On the top of this mountain there is a large mark. People say this is Gotama Buddha's footprint. Visitors climb to see it, often at sunrise.

Offerings

At places of pilgrimage, Buddhists offer flowers, incense and light.

Learning from pilgrimage

Buddhist believe in rebirth. Visiting holy places helps them achieve a better rebirth. That means a next life which will bring them closer to enlightenment. What makes a pilgrimage special is what it does to the inner life of a person. Many people find they can concentrate better on the Buddha's teachings when they are away from their normal lives.

> **New words**
>
> stupa

C Pilgrims at Sri Pada in Sri Lanka

THINGS TO DO

1 Use the photographs and text in this unit to help you. Describe in your own words:
   • what pilgrims find at Bodh Gaya
   • the pilgrimage to Sri Pada.

2 Any place connected with the life of the Buddha is interesting to Buddhists. Why do you think some places became more important than others? Look back in the text to help you.

3 Gotama Buddha gained enlightenment at Bodh Gaya. Perhaps you have heard sayings like, 'Can you enlighten me?' or 'I've seen the light'. Try to make a list of other sayings about light. Explain in your own words what each one means.

4 Being on top of the mountain at Sri Pada to see the sun rise can be very inspiring. Choose one of the following:
   a Write a story or a poem about something else that might inspire people or
   b Make a poster or booklet of pictures that might stir up strong feelings

23

The spread of Christianity

Christians are followers of **Jesus Christ**. They believe he is the Son of God. Jesus was a Jew. He was born in Israel in about 6 BCE.

A Jesus' baptism shown in a stained glass window

Jesus' Baptism

When he was about 30 Jesus was **baptized** in the River Jordan by a powerful preacher called John (**A**). Going into the water was a symbol of a new start. Jews at that time were expecting a king to set up God's kingdom on earth. Christians believe John recognized Jesus as the king they had been waiting for. He is sometimes called the Messiah or the Christ. Messiah means 'anointed'.'Christ' is the Greek work for Messiah. All kings were **anointed** with oil when they were crowned.

Jesus the teacher

After his baptism, Jesus became a travelling teacher. He had twelve followers called **disciples**. Many other people came to hear what he had to say as well. Christians believe he cared about the poor and unpopular people. He healed the sick. He taught that God loved everyone.

The birth of Christianity

Jesus was not popular with everyone. After teaching for about three years he was **crucified**. He died hanging on a cross.

Jesus' followers believe he rose from the dead (see unit 28). They were inspired to carry on teaching his message.
The number of followers grew quickly. They became known as Christians.

Christianity grows

The teachings of Jesus and his followers were written down. They are found in the **Gospels** and other books of the Christian **New Testament**. Christianity spread to countries all round the Mediterranean Sea. By the sixth century it had reached Britain. Today it is found in all countries. About a third of the people in the world claim to be Christians.

In the late twentieth century Christianity grew most quickly in Africa and Latin

America. This means that most Christians are black (**B**). The most common language is Spanish (**C**).

Discussion question

Being persecuted does not stop people believing in their religion. In fact it often makes people's faith stronger. Can you suggest why this might be true?

Christianity around the world

From early times Christians have worshipped in different ways. There are now many different groups of Christians. These are called **denominations** of the Church.

New words

Jesus Christ   baptized   anointed
disciples   crucified   Gospels
New Testament   denominations

B Black Christians at worship

C The most widely spoken language amongst Christians is Spanish

THINGS TO DO

1 In the time of Jesus, Jews were expecting a king to set up God's kingdom on earth. Christians believe Jesus came to do this. However, he lived as a travelling teacher. How could Jesus set up God's kingdom by teaching people? In what ways can teachers be said to have power?

2 Christians believe Jesus cared for everyone. He looked after the outcasts – people no one else liked. Who are the outcasts in our society today? Many Christians believe they should follow Jesus' example in helping people like these. How might believing this affect their everyday lives? How could they help such people?

3 Christians believe Jesus told his followers to teach other people about him. How do you think Christians today could teach other people about Jesus and his message?

4 Do you have ideas or beliefs which are important to you? Are there any which are so important that you would not give them up for anything? Try to explain why you feel the way you do.

24

Symbols in Christianity

The cross

The best known Christian symbol is the **cross**. This is because Jesus died on a cross. This can be a picture, an object or an action. People make the sign of the cross by touching their forehead, chest and shoulders.

Symbols in worship

In many churches Christians break bread and drink wine to remind them of when Jesus did this at his last supper.

Some churches use many symbols in worship. They can help believers concentrate on spiritual things.

In **Orthodox churches** there are **icons** (**A**). These are holy pictures of Christ, **Mary** and the saints. **Roman Catholic** churches often have statues of Mary and other saints. Saints are people who have dedicated their lives to God. Some people pray to Mary because they believe she can talk to Jesus for them.

Other churches have little or no decoration. Some Christians believe that symbols distract people from their worship. In a **Society of Friends** meeting house there is no decoration (**B**). People meet to be silent and share thoughts.

Discussion question

Do you think you would prefer a plain or highly decorated place for worship? Why?

A Orthodox churches are often highly decorated

B A Society of Friends meeting house is very simple

Water

Many Christian denominations use water for baptisms. This is when people are welcomed into the Christian family. Some Churches put water in a font to baptize babies. Others baptize new believers. These are people who have decided for themselves to live as Christians. They dip their whole body in water. This is a sign that their old lives have ended. They are beginning new lives with Christ.

Signs of belonging

Many Christians use symbols to show they belong to the faith. Members of the **Salvation Army** wear a uniform with a badge (**C**). Others wear a cross or **crucifix** as a necklace. Some wear a fish brooch or pin. The Greek word for fish is made up of the letters ICTHUS. These are the the first letters of the words 'Jesus Christ God's Son Saviour'.

C Members of the Salvation Army wear a uniform with a badge to show they are Christians

THINGS TO DO

1 Look at the differences between the two churches in Photos **A** and **B**. Imagine you each go to one of these churches. Describe the place of worship. Explain why it looks as it does.

2 Do you wear uniforms or badges to show you belong to any groups? Why do you think some people choose to use symbols to show they are Christians? Can you think of any difficulties they might have because they make their religion very obvious?

3 When someone is baptized it shows that the person wants to live as a Christian. How might making the decision public be helpful or cause difficulties for a new Christian?

4 Choose some Christian symbols. Make a poster showing and explaining each one. You might like to look up more information in books, on CD-ROMs and the Internet.

New words

cross   Orthodox churches   icons
Mary   Roman Catholic
Society of Friends   Salvation Army
crucifix

25

Adam and Eve

Some Christians believe this story describes exactly what happened. Others think it is a story with a message.

The Garden of Eden

God made Adam and Eve. He breathed life into them. He put them in a special garden. They were to care for it. There were plenty of trees with fruit to eat. Right in the middle of the garden God put two special trees. One was the Tree of Knowledge of Good and Evil. God told Adam and Eve that they must not eat the fruit from this tree. If they did they would die.

Temptation

The cunning serpent asked Eve what God had said about the Tree of Knowledge of Good and Evil. She told him that if they ate its fruit they would die. The serpent said this was not true. He said if they ate the fruit they would know the difference between good and evil.

The fruit looked good. Eve took some and ate it. She gave some to Adam. Suddenly, they saw things differently. For the first time they noticed they were naked. They made clothes out of leaves to cover themselves.

Discussion question

Do you think it is always easy to tell the difference between good and evil? Explain why you think as you do.

Punishment

Adam and Eve hid from God. He asked why they were hiding. Adam said, 'I was

A God cursed the serpent

naked and afraid so I hid from you.' God asked, 'Who said you were naked? Have you eaten the fruit from the tree that I told you not to eat?'

'The woman made me do it,' Adam answered. Eve said, 'The serpent tricked me into eating the fruit.' God was disappointed and angry. He cursed the serpent. It would now always go about on its belly and be an enemy to man and woman (**A**).

Woman was punished as well. Every time she had a child it would be painful. Man would have to earn his bread through endless hard work and effort (**B** and **C**). Man and woman could not escape death.

B Adam would have to work hard to survive

God had made them from the dust and they would become dust again. God had them turned out of the Garden of Eden.

C Man and woman would suffer as a result of their disobedience

THINGS TO DO

1 In the story, God made Adam and Eve perfect in a perfect world. He gave them freedom to choose how to behave. Some people say this story explains how evil and suffering came into God's perfect world. It was because the first people did not obey God. Do you think this is a good explanation? Give reasons for your answer.

2 Christians believe that because of this story no one has been able to live a completely good life. Why do you think people often choose to do wrong rather than good?

3 Adam and Eve gave in to temptation. We have all been tempted to do something we know we should not do. Make up a story called 'The Temptation'. You can tell it in words or pictures or act it out.

4 Both Adam and Eve passed the blame for what they did on to someone else. Many people find it hard to accept responsibility for their own actions. Why is this often a hard thing to do? Do you think people should accept responsibility for their own actions? Give reasons for your answer.

26

The Christian Year

Christian festivals remind believers of the life of Christ and give them time to think about it.

Advent

During **Advent** Christians prepare for **Christmas**. They think about how God sent his son to be born on earth. God loved people so much that he sent his son to help put things right between people and God.

Advent means 'coming'. Christians think about the coming of Jesus in the story of his birth. Candles help remind them of Jesus as the 'Light of the World' (**A**). Some people also think about Jesus' promise to come again at the end of time.

A An Advent wreath being lit in church

Lent

Lent is the time to prepare for **Easter**. It used to be a time of strict fasting. Today many Christians give up something. Some still **fast**. They test themselves. This reminds them of the time Jesus went into the wilderness and was tempted. He did not give in.

During Lent many Christians pray and study their religion more than usual. It is a time of repentance. They ask God to forgive them for things they have done wrong.

Discussion question

Fasting is one way of putting yourself to the test. Can you think of times when you have put yourself to the test in some way? Can you explain why you did it and how you felt about it?

Holy Week

The last week of Lent is Holy Week. Christians think about the last week of Jesus' life. On Palm Sunday Jesus rode into Jerusalem. He was greeted like a king. People waved palm branches. Today palm crosses are given out in many churches.

On Maundy Thursday, Christians remember the last supper Jesus had with his disciples. He broke bread and asked them to do this to remember him. He also said,

'Love one another. As I have loved you, so you must love one another.
(John 13:34).

In some churches feet are washed as a sign of service to others (**B**).

Good Friday is the day on which Christians remember the death of Jesus. Some churches are decorated with purple cloths. Many Roman Catholic Christians pray before the **Stations of the Cross**.

B On Maunday Thursday feet are washed in some churches. This is a sign of service to others.

In some Orthodox churches, the priest carries in an icon of the body of Jesus. People look on as if they were at a funeral. Christians think about how they believe Jesus died to save the world from sin (**C**).

C Jesus died to save the world from sin

New words

Advent   Christmas   Lent   Easter
fast   Stations of the Cross

THINGS TO DO

1 Jesus told his disciples to call him Lord and Teacher. He said that even though he was their teacher it was right for him to wash their feet as though he was a servant. He said they should follow this example. What do you think this tells Christians about how they should behave?

2 Many Christians pray and study their religion all through the year. They do this more than usual at Advent and Lent. How do you think this helps them prepare for the festivals of Christmas and Easter? What things do you prepare for? How do you prepare?

3 Christians are told to love one another as Jesus loves them. In groups discuss what this might mean in everyday life.

4 Make a list of all the festivals mentioned in this unit. Beside each one explain what the festival celebrates or remembers. You could set this out like a chart.

Christmas

Christmas is a time of celebration almost all over the world. For Christians it is a very religious time. People who follow no religion and some people who follow other religions also enjoy Christmas. For them it is a family time when presents are exchanged.

Discussion question

Christmas is a Christian festival. Why do you think people who are not Christians also celebrate it?

The birth of Jesus

Christians believe God was born into the world in Jesus. The story of Jesus' birth is found in the Gospels of Matthew and Luke. Many Christians believe they describe exactly what happened. Others believe that the lessons taught by the stories are more important.

They show Jesus was born in a stable. His parents were ordinary people. The first people to visit the stable were shepherds. When more important visitors arrived they were from another country. Christians believe these things show God's gift was for everyone no matter who they are.

The Light of the World

Lights are used at Christmas. They are used to show the idea that Jesus is the 'Light of the World' (A). His teachings light the way to understanding God. Some people say the lights are to light the darkness of winter. This is not the real reason, because for Christians in some parts of the world Christmas comes in summer (B).

Epiphany

Epiphany comes at the end of Christmas. It is when many Christians remember when the **magi** or wise men visited Jesus. For Orthodox Christians it also celebrates Jesus' baptism and first **miracle**.

A Christmas tree lights remind Christians that Jesus is the Light of the World

B In many countries Christmas is celebrated in the warm summer months

Christians at work

Christmas reminds Christians that God showed himself in the world. It is now up to them to do God's work in the world. They must live as Jesus taught them. Many make a special effort at Christmas to help others. They might sing carols or provide meals and shelter for the poor (**C**). They might promise to try to live a better Christian life.

C Christmas is a time when Christians make a special effort to care for others

New words

magi   miracle

THINGS TO DO

1 Some people complain that Christmas is just a time for people to make money. They say the Christian meaning of Christmas has been lost. What do you think about this? Should the Christian message be clearer for everyone at Christmas? Work in groups. Each group should prepare a statement about their views. These can be read in turn to the whole class.

2 At Epiphany Christians remember the magi visiting the stable to see Jesus. They gave him gifts – gold, frankincense and myrrh. Many Christians believe these are symbols of Jesus as a king, as God and of his important death.
When we give gifts they should be just right for the person we are giving them to. Think of three people you know. Decide on a gift for each one. Say what you have chosen and why.

3 At Christmas, even more than usual, Christians try to help others.
Choose one of these things to do:
• Make a collage to show the kinds of ways Christians might help others at Christmas
• Find out what local Christians do to help others at Christmas in your area.

4. Design a symbol to show the idea that Jesus is the Light of the World. Remember that Christians believe that Jesus brought light to the whole world and everyone in it. Explain your symbol when it is finished.

28

Easter

'Christ is risen.' These words are said in many churches on Easter morning.

Symbols of Easter

The joy of Easter is shown in church services. The Orthodox Church has a service very late on Saturday night. It lasts until Sunday morning. Everyone has a candle. Candles light the building. At midnight everyone goes outside. The doors are shut. The church is in complete darkness. This reminds people of Jesus' tomb. Then the priest says, 'Christ is risen.' The people reply, 'He is risen indeed.' The doors are opened. This makes people think of the stone being rolled away from the tomb. Inside all the lights are shining (**A**).

Where it is spring, flowers are used in churches as a sign of new life.

Resurrection

Christians believe that after he died Jesus came back to life. This is called the resurrection. They believe that Jesus is still with them today. This does not mean that their lives will be easy. They will not always be happy. Christians will still have problems, difficulties and sadness. The difference is they believe Jesus is with them to help them through. This helps Christians look forward with hope.

The cathedral in Coventry is a symbol of hope. The city was bombed in the Second World War. The cathedral was destroyed. People could have stayed bitter and kept their feelings of hatred. However, a new cathedral was built. This was a symbol of Christian forgiveness and hope for a new future (**B** and **C**).

God's work

When Christians follow the teachings of Jesus they are showing God's love in the

A An Orthodox church on Easter Saturday. Everyone has a candle

B & C Coventry Cathedral has become a symbol of Christian hope and forgiveness

world. They believe they are doing God's work just like Jesus did. They are showing other people what Jesus was like by living their lives as he taught them.

Discussion question

The Church is sometimes called the 'Body of Christ'. What do you think this means? How can Christians be like Jesus' hands, eyes, ears and so on?

Life after death

Christians believe everyone does wrong things. This means they could not live with God who is perfect. Christians say Jesus died so that everyone's sins would be taken away. When he rose from the dead he showed there was life after death. The message of Easter is that Christians will live a perfect life with God after death.

THINGS TO DO

1 What does this unit tell you about how Christians understand life? Prepare a short radio programme about how believing in the resurrection affects the way Christians think about life.

2 Design an Easter symbol or poster. It must show Christian beliefs about the death and resurrection of Christ.

3 Every religion says something about life after death. The last section of this unit tells you a little about the Christian idea. What do you think about this? What other beliefs about life after death have you heard?

4 Find out who in your class celebrates Easter and what they do.

29

Ascension and Pentecost

Ascension

Christians believe Jesus met with his friends after he rose from the dead. On Ascension Day they remember when Christ left his followers for the last time. He returned to God. He told them to carry on with his work. He promised the **Holy Spirit** would come to them. This would be God's presence on earth.

Pentecost

Later the disciples were in Jerusalem to celebrate the Jewish festival of Shavuot or Pentecost. They had gathered together in a room. The story says the Spirit came like a rush of wind. It settled on the disciples like flames. After this they found they could speak in tongues. This was a special way of communicating. They could speak in languages they did not know. Pilgrims from all over the place could understand when they spoke.

People were excited when they heard about Jesus. Many decided to join the disciples. As a sign, they were baptized. Many people say this was the beginning, or birth, of the Christian Church.

It became a custom for Christians to be baptized at Pentecost They used to wear white so it became known as White Sunday. Eventually this became Whitsun.

Guiding Christians today

After that Pentecost experience the disciples were changed. They had courage to carry on Jesus' teaching. Christians believe they were changed by the Holy Spirit. Many believe the Holy Spirit is with them today. He guides their lives and the work of the Church.

A Christians praise God in a Pentecostal Church

B Christians use their skills to serve God

Discussion question

How do you think Christians can tell that it is the Holy Spirit guiding them? How do they know it is not just their own ideas?

Gifts

Christians believe people are given different talents and skills. They can use these to serve and praise God in different ways (**A**&**B**).

Symbols

Symbols help people understand the Holy Spirit (**C**). At Jesus' baptism it came down as a dove. At Pentecost it came as wind and fire.

New words

Holy Spirit

C A banner to illustrate Pentecost

THINGS TO DO

1   Many Christians through the years believe they have been changed by the Holy Spirit. Lots of people have experiences which change them. Think up a story about an experience like this. It can be true or made up. Write or act out your story.

2   What do you think the symbols of wind, breath, fire and a dove teach Christians about the Holy Spirit? Look carefully at Photo **C**. It is a banner in Winchester Cathedral. How can people tell it is about Pentecost? Do you think it is a good symbol for Pentecost? Give reasons for your answer.

3   Work in groups. Think about the skills and talents of each person in your group. How could these gifts be used in the service of God? Make up a diagram to show your ideas.

4   Christians believe the Holy Spirit is always with them. What effect might this have on them?

30

Christian pilgrimage

There are places of Christian pilgrimage in many countries.

Israel

One of the most famous places of Christian pilgrimage is Israel. It was where Jesus lived. Many Christians like to visit places where Jesus went.

At Easter lots of pilgrims go to Jerusalem. This is where Jesus died and rose to new life. Crowds walk along the Via Dolorosa or 'Way of Sorrow' (**A**). People say this is the way Jesus went to the place where he was crucified. It helps them think about what happened to Jesus.

Walsingham in Britain

Christian pilgrims also travel to Walsingham in Norfolk. In 1061, Lady Richeldis had a vision of the Virgin Mary, the mother of Jesus. A spring of water appeared. A simple church was built. Today about 250,000 people visit Walsingham each year.

Lourdes in France

Lourdes became a place of pilgrimage in a similar way. In 1858 a girl called Bernadette Soubirous had a vision of Mary. A spring appeared. At first no one believed Bernadette's story. Later, Christians started to visit Lourdes. The spring water is said to have healing powers. Many of the pilgrims who go to Lourdes are ill (**B**). Not many of them are cured but the place seems to give lots of them a feeling of peace. Some pilgrims say that after going to Lourdes they feel stronger inside.

A Pilgrims on the Via Dolorosa

B Many pilgrims to Lourdes have a feeling of great peace there

C The Pope giving his blessing in St Peter's Square, Rome

Rome

One of the reasons that Christian pilgrims go to Rome is that Saint Peter died there. He was one of the **apostles** of Jesus. The Romans tried to stop him spreading the Christian message. He would not, so he was killed. People believe his tomb is under St Peter's Church in Rome.

This part of Rome is now called the **Vatican**. It is the centre of the Roman Catholic Church. At special times the **Pope** blesses the crowds that gather in St Peter's Square (**C**).

Stronger faith

Many Christians believe the important thing about pilgrimage is that it can help make their faith stronger.

New words

apostles   Vatican   Pope

THINGS TO DO

1 Make a leaflet to advertise an Easter pilgrimage to Israel. It should tell people where they will go and how this might help their Christian faith.

2 Most Christians would say travelling to places is not the most important thing about pilgrimage. More important is what goes on inside the pilgrim. They might come to understand Christian beliefs better. Explain in your own words how studying, praying and meditating could take a person on a spiritual journey.

3 Many Christians believe God still makes miracles happen. What do you think? Discuss your ideas in your class.

4 St Peter's strong faith was an example for Christians to follow. Think of someone you admire. Explain why this person is special and what have you learned from their example or what they have said.

31 Islam: roots and origins

People like to know the story of their family and their past. Each religion tells a story about its past and how it all began.

Muslims trace the beginnings of their religion back to the first human being. They believe this was Adam. **Islam** teaches that Adam was the first man and the first **Muslim**.

The will of Allah

The word Islam means peace. It also means submission or giving in. A Muslim is someone who gives in to the will of Allah (**A**). Allah is the Muslim word for God. Muslims believe everyone is born with a choice. One choice is to follow selfish desire and greed. The other is to follow the straight path that leads to peace. This path is the will of Allah.

Discussion question

Do you believe that everyone is free to choose their own path in life?

The prophets

According to the story of Islam, Adam was the first person to follow the will of Allah. He was also the first in a line of **prophets**. A prophet is someone who has received guidance from God.

A A Muslim is someone who submits to the will of Allah

64

Ādam	Adam
Idrīs	*Enoch*
Nūḥ	*Noah*
Hūd	—
Ṣāliḥ	*Salih*
Ibrāhīm	*Abraham*
Ismā'il	*Ishmael*
Isḥāq	*Isaac*
Lūṭ	*Lot*
Ya'qūb	*Jacob*
Yūsuf	*Joseph*
Shu'aib	—
Ayyūb	*Job*
Mūsā	*Moses*
Hārūn	*Aaron*
Dhū'l-kifl	*Ezekiel*
Dāwūd	*David*
Sulaimān	*Solomon*
Iliās	*Elias*
Al-Yasā'	*Elisha*
Yūnus	*Jonah*
Zakariyyā	*Zechariah*
Yaḥyā	*John*
'Īsā	*Jesus*
Muḥammad	—

B The prophets and messengers of Allah

Muslims believe that since the beginning of time Allah has sent his messengers and prophets to every nation and every age (**B**). All the prophets of Allah have given the same message. That is to worship Allah. Muslims believe Allah is the One True God and there is no god but Allah.

Muhammad

Muhammad was the last and final prophet according to the teachings of Islam. He was born in **Makkah** in what is now Saudi Arabia (**C**). It was here in the mountains outside Makkah that Muhammad received the words of the **Qur'an**. Muslims believe that the Qur'an contains the word of Allah. It is his final and complete **revelation**.

New words

Islam   Muslim   Allah   prophets
Muhammad   Makkah   Qur'an
revelation

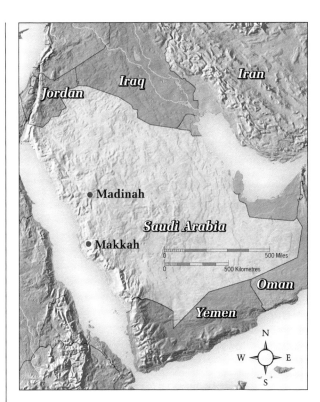

C Saudi Arabia showing Makkah where Muhammad was born

THINGS TO DO

1 Draw a diagram to show the two choices that Muslims believe are open to everyone.

2 Write down two things you are free to choose in life. Write down two things that are chosen for you. Is it good that some things are decided for you? Write your answer and give your reasons.

3 Draw a map of Saudi Arabia showing where Makkah is. Say in one sentence why this place is important in the history of Islam.

4 Muslims look back through history to prophets and messengers who have been important. Draw up your own list of important people who have made your life better or the world a better place.

32 The story of Muhammad

Muhammad was born in 571 CE. His family belonged to a powerful tribe in Makkah called the Quraish. His father died before he was born. His mother died when he was six. Muhammad lived with his grandfather until he was eight. He then lived with his uncle, Abu Talib.

Muhammad's early life

Muhammad looked after his uncle's sheep when he was young. Later he helped in the family business. He was called 'trustworthy'. A businesswoman called Khadijah asked him to run her trading company. Muhammad made the business a success. Khadijah asked him to marry her. Muhammad said yes.

Muhammad liked to think deeply about life. Some things in Makkah made him sad. The leaders were bad and did not care about the people. They just wanted power. This often led to people fighting. The poor and the needy were forgotten.

Muhammad did not like the way people forgot about God. In Makkah there was a shrine called the **Ka'bah** (**A**). This was the place where **Ibrahim** had first worshipped the one True God. Now people only worshipped **idols** there.

The angel Jibril

Muhammad sometimes liked to be alone. One day when he was praying the angel

Discussion question

What things do you think would make Muhammad sad and depressed if he were alive today (**B**)?

A The Ka'bah in Makkah

B Do people still ignore the needs of the poor and is there corruption today?

Jibril appeared. He commanded Muhammad to read. Muhammad said, 'I can't read'. The angel hugged him and said again, 'Read'. Muhammad said again, 'I can't read'. Once more the angel squeezed him and said:

'Read in the name of your Lord who created.
Created man from a clot of blood.
Read, your Lord is most Generous.
Who taught by the pen.
Taught man what he did not know.'
(Qur'an 96:1-5)

Muhammad found the words came to him. These were the first words of the Qur'an. The Qur'an is the holy book for for Muslims. Muhammad received many more visits from the angel. Muslims believe that the words he brought to Muhammed came from God.

New words

Ka'bah   Ibrahim   idols

THINGS TO DO

1 Muslims do not draw pictures of the prophets. This is so that they do not make idols. Take one section of the story of Muhammad and design a page for a children's book which has words and pictures. Remember – no people in your drawing!

2 Muhammad did not like the way people made things like idols and then worshipped them. Make a poster to show the sort of things that people worship today. For example, you could include money, cars, and televisions.

3 Muhammad wanted the world to be a fairer and better place. What things would make the world a better place today? Write your thoughts in a letter to a newspaper.

4 Muhammad liked to be alone in the mountains. What special place do you have where you like to be alone? Why is it special?

33

Signs, symbols and beliefs

One God

Muslims believe in one God called Allah. Allah is Eternal and Absolute and there is none like Him. The belief in the Oneness of Allah is called **tawhid**. Muslims believe that Allah is all-knowing, all-wise and all-powerful. Allah can see everything but no one can see Allah. It is a sin to try to show Allah in a picture or image. In **mosques** where Muslims worship there are no images or pictures. There are only patterns (**A**). These may have words from the Qur'an instead of pictures.

Allah is merciful, Allah is kind. Muslims use qualities like these to describe Allah. Some Muslims recite the 99 beautiful names of Allah as a form of worship.

No images

There is no image of Allah for followers to see. But Muslims do not need one. Allah has told them everything they need to know about Him in the Qur'an (**B**). The Qur'an is a symbol of Allah's great love towards men and women. It is therefore treated with great respect.

Some signs and symbols are important for Muslims. For example, in the mosque, there is a small arch in the wall called the **mihrab**. This is a sign of the direction of Makkah. All Muslims face the direction of the Ka'bah in Makkah for prayer.

A Geometric designs and words from the Qur'an are used to decorate the walls of the mosque

B The Qur'an contains the words of Allah and is therefore treated with great respect

C Muslim prayer positions express humility and obedience

The Ka'bah

The Ka'bah is an important symbol for Muslims. It reminds them of the faith of Ibrahim. According to the Qur'an, Allah tested Ibrahim.

Discussion question

Shared symbols can be a sign of unity and togetherness. One example might be a school badge. What other examples can you give?

Allah asked Ibrahim to offer the life of his son as a sacrifice. Ibrahim was willing to do this. But just as he was about to kill his son, Allah stopped him and provided a ram instead. Ibrahim and his son built the Ka'bah. It is a symbol of perfect faith and obedience.

How Muslims pray

Muslims wash before prayer as a sign of respect. This is called **wudu**. Muslims bow right down when they pray (**C**). When they pray together at the mosque they stand shoulder to shoulder. This is a sign of equality and brotherhood. Everyone is equal before God.

New words

tawhid   mosques   mihrab   wudu

THINGS TO DO

1 Design an information sheet on three important signs or symbols in Islam.

2 The crescent moon is often seen as a symbol for Islam. It represents the calendar that Muslims follow which is based on the cycle of the moon. If you wanted a symbol to show perfect faith, what would you choose? Design and explain a symbol.

3 Design a patterned border to go round the border of your work on Islam.

4 If you wanted to encourage the idea that everyone is equal in school what rules and activities would you introduce? Explain your answer in writing.

34

The Creation in Islam

Discussion question

What examples of pattern or design can you find in nature? Are these a sign of a God or creator?

Muslims believe that it is possible to see the work of Allah by looking at the world around us.

The sun provides daylight. The moon serves the night. Spring follows winter (**A**). Everything follows a pattern and an order. Muslims believe that in nature everything follows the will of Allah.

Created by Allah

Muslims believe that men and women were created by Allah like everything else.

A Spring follows winter and flowers blossom according to their time

But men and women have free choice. They do not have to follow the will of Allah. So the human world is full of disorder (**B**).

Adam was the first to obey Allah. Over the years men and women forgot Allah and worshipped idols. They began to lie, cheat and steal. They became greedy and selfish.

The prophet Nuh

Allah sent **Nuh**, a great prophet, to bring the people back to Him. No one listened to Nuh. So Allah asked Nuh to build an **ark**. Allah was going to send a great flood to cover the earth.

When the ark was ready, Nuh took one male and one female of each of the animals on the earth. He gathered those who believed in Allah and took them on board the ark.

The Storm

The clouds gathered and the rains fell. It rained and rained until the earth was covered in water. Every living creature was drowned except those who were in the ark. The floods lasted five months.

Reaching dry land

At last the skies cleared. The ark reached Mount Judi. Nuh and all those in the ark set foot on dry land again. They lived in peace on earth and followed the will of Allah.

New words

Nuh   ark

B Refugees flee to safety: it is only in the world of human affairs that there is confusion and disorder

C Muslim children learn stories about the prophets

THINGS TO DO

1 What examples of pattern and harmony can you find in the world? For example, the balance between night and day, or the pattern of the crystals in a snowflake. Design a poster to show the Muslim belief that the patterns and harmony in nature are a sign that God created the world.

2 Tell the story of Nuh in words and pictures. Avoid drawing the prophet Nuh. Can you say why?

3 The world after the flood was a perfect world. What is your idea of a perfect world? Write a description in your own words.

4 Stories about the prophets help Muslims to learn about right and wrong (**C**). What stories do you know that tell you what is right and what is wrong? Explain one story in your own words.

35 Ramadan and Id-ul-Fitr

Ramadan

Every year during the month of **Ramadan** Muslims have a duty to **fast**. Ramadan falls at a different time each year. This is because Muslims follow a calendar based on the cycle of the moon.

Fasting

During the fast, Muslims must not eat or drink during the hours of daylight. They get up early to eat before dawn. Once the sun has gone down, they can break the fast and eat again (**B**). In the summer, when the days are long and hot, Ramadan is very hard. The very young and the very old do not have to fast. Pregnant women and those who are ill do not fast either.

Reasons for fasting

There are several reasons for the fast. Going without food helps Muslims to learn what it is like to be very poor and hungry. Fasting builds self-discipline. Muslims learn to put the will of Allah before their own wants and needs.

Discussion question

What is the difference between fasting and dieting?

Ramadan is not dull or gloomy. There is a sense of community because people are sharing the same experience. Muslims try to help one another. They forgive each other. There is more time to go to the mosque and study the Qur'an (**A**).

The festival of Id-ul-Fitr

At the end of Ramadan is a festival called **Id-ul-Fitr** which means festival of fast

A Ramadan is a time to study the Qur'an

B Every night when the fast is broken the family meal is like a small celebration

breaking. It is a time of celebration. Everyone goes to the mosque for prayers. Families share a festive meal and children get new clothes. People give money to the poor. This giving is called **Zakat-ul-Fitr**. Id-ul-Fitr is a time of joy and peace.

Fast ends	Fast begins	1997 Jan/Feb	1417 Ramadan	Days
4.13	6.32	10	1	Fri
4.15	6.31	11	2	Sat
4.16	6.31	12	3	Sun
4.18	6.30	13	4	Mon
4.20	6.30	14	5	Tue
4.21	6.29	15	6	Wed
4.23	6.28	16	7	Thur
4.25	6.28	17	8	Fri
4.27	6.27	18	9	Sat
4.28	6.26	19	10	Sun
4.30	6.25	20	11	Mon
4.32	6.24	21	12	Tue
4.34	6.23	22	13	Wed
4.36	6.22	23	14	Thur
4.38	6.21	24	15	Fri
4.39	6.20	25	16	Sat
4.41	6.19	26	17	Sun
4.43	6.18	27	18	Mon
4.45	6.17	28	19	Tue
4.47	6.15	29	20	Wed
4.49	6.14	30	21	Thur
4.51	6.13	31	22	Fri
4.53	6.11	1	23	Sat
4.55	6.10	2	24	Sun
4.57	6.08	3	25	Mon
4.59	6.07	4	26	Tue
5.01	6.05	5	27	Wed
5.03	6.04	6	28	Thur
5.07	6.02	7	29	Fri
5.09	6.01	8	30	Sat

C A UK timetable for the fast of Ramadan: it reads from right to left

New words

fast   Ramadan   Id-ul-Fitr   Zakat-ul-Fitr

THINGS TO DO

1 Look at the timetable for Ramadan (**C**). Work out when Muslims will have breakfast during this month. Now work out the earliest time that a Muslim could have their evening meal in this month.

2 Draw a circle to show a typical day in Ramadan. Use the timetable to help you. Shade out the hours of darkness. Fill in times a Muslim might go to the mosque, pray, read the Qur'an, break their fast and have a meal.

3 Ramadan is a time for moral and spiritual growth. Write down which of the following activities might help you to grow morally or spiritually and which would not.
   • shopping
   • reading a good book
   • listening to music
   • helping someone
   • dancing
   • playing cards
   • singing
   • walking in the countryside
   • playing computer games.

Make your own list of activities that you think would help spiritual development.

4 Remembering the hungry is important. Why? How could you make schoolchildren more aware of the needs of the poor and hungry? Write your answer.

36

The Hajj

Hajj is the Muslim **pilgrimage** to Makkah. A Muslim must make this pilgrimage once in their life if they can afford it.

For Muslims Makkah is a holy city. The Ka'bah is there. It was built by the prophet Ibrahim. At the time of Muhammad the people had forgotten the faith of Ibrahim. They had started to worship idols. It was Muhammad who made the Ka'bah a centre for worshipping Allah again.

From Makkah to Madinah

When Muhammad began to preach, people started to follow him. The city leaders did not like this. They tried to get rid of Muhammad. He moved to Madinah where the people made him their leader.

He set up the first Muslim community there. The Makkans tried to destroy the community. Muhammad returned to Makkah with an army of 10,000. The city was unable to put up a fight. So Muhammad declared peace and forgave the Makkans.

The Ka'bah was cleared of idols and dedicated to Allah. Makkah became a city of peace.

Discussion question

What would you expect to find in a city of peace?

Preparations for the Hajj

Muslims prepare carefully for the Hajj. Before arriving in Makkah they wash and put on special clothes called **ihram** (**A**). These are two pieces of white cloth.

A Pilgrims wear ihram as a sign of equality

B Pilgrims at the Ka'bah

Everyone is dressed the same. This is a sign of equality.

On the Hajj, Muslims first visit the Ka'bah. They perform **tawaf** which means walking round the Ka'bah seven times (**B**). They then go to visit two hills called Safa and Marwah. The Qur'an says that Ibrahim's wife, Hajar, ran between these hills searching for water for her son Isma'il. Isma'il scuffed his foot and a spring of water appeared. This spring is called Zamzam.

A time of peace

For the next stage, pilgrims travel to Arafat where Muhammad gave his last sermon. He asked Allah to forgive the sins of all believers. At Arafat Muslims stand in silent prayer. They ask for forgiveness and the strength to forgive others. Hajj is a time of peace.

THINGS TO DO

1 Draw the Ka'bah and say why it is special for Muslims.

2 Forgiveness is important. Peace begins with forgiveness. Write a short story to show this.

3 In the desert water marks a special place. Do you think we take water for granted? Design a poster to show the wonder of water.

4 Design and write a postcard that a Muslim might send home from the Hajj.

New words

Hajj   pilgrimage   ihram   tawaf

37

Id-ul-Adha

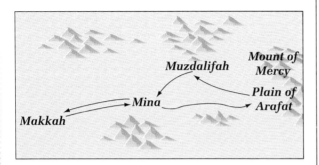

A The route taken by pilgrims on the Hajj

The Hajj takes place in Dhul-Hijrah, the twelfth month of the Muslim calendar.

There are different stages to the Hajj (**A**). At Arafat (**B**) Muslims are reminded of the mercy of Allah. They come away feeling forgiven and at peace with others. The next stage prepares them for going back into the world with all its temptations.

At sundown pilgrims travel to Muzdalifah outside Makkah and stay the night there. Before they sleep, pilgrims gather small stones ready for the next day when they go to Mina.

The struggle against evil

At Mina there are three stone pillars. These are a sign of the powers of **Shaytan**. Muslims believe that Shaytan tempted

B At Arafat Muslims ask Allah for forgiveness

importance of perfect faith and obedience to Allah.

Many families offer a goat or sheep at Id-ul-Adha. It is killed as set out in Islamic law. The meat is prepared for a shared meal. The rest is given to the poor (**C**).

Muslims must be willing to give up everything for Allah just as Ibrahim was willing to give up his son.

Id-ul-Adha is a time for family and friends to get together. It is celebrated by all Muslims everywhere.

New words

Shaytan   Id-ul-Adha

C At Id-ul-Adha some of the meat is shared out. The rest is given to the poor

Ibrahim and tried to persuade him to turn away from Allah. Pilgrims throw stones at the pillars. This shows that they mean to fight against evil and temptation in their lives.

The festival of Id-ul-Adha

After this pilgrims wash and cut their hair and dress in their usual clothes. The pilgrimage ends with **Id-ul-Adha**. This is the festival of sacrifice. It reminds Muslims of the time when Ibrahim was about to offer his son as a sacrifice to Allah. The Qur'an tells them that Allah gave him a ram to sacrifice instead. Id-ul Adha is a time to remember the

THINGS TO DO

1 Write down three different thoughts and feelings that a Muslim might have as they get ready to leave Mina.

2 Draw a map showing the different sites of the Hajj. Explain one of the special places on the map.

3 Giving up something that is precious to us is a hard lesson. Describe something precious to you that you would not want to give up.

4 Muslims call the voice of temptation Shaytan. Draw a person who is being tempted. Write in the speech bubble the voice of temptation. Write in another bubble their efforts to say no to temptation.

38

Sikhism: The story of Guru Nanak

Sikhs look to **Guru Nanak** as the founder of their faith. Guru Nanak was born in 1469 CE in a village called Talwandi in the Punjab. This was once in India. It is now in Pakistan (**A**). He was born into a Hindu family. The majority of people in India were Hindu. However, the people in power at the time were Muslims.

The early life of Guru Nanak

Guru Nanak was an unusual child. He spent much of his time in prayer and meditation. His father had high hopes for his future.

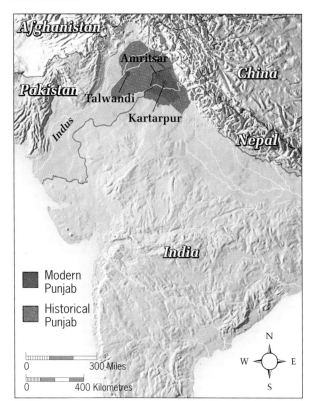

A Guru Nanak was born in the Punjab in the north of the Indian subcontinent

Modern Punjab

Historical Punjab

0   300 Miles
0   400 Kilometres

N
W   E
S

B Every day Guru Nanak would spend time meditating

But Guru Nanak was more interested in talking with holy men than in making a career. He was sad to see that religious leaders were not helping the people get close to God. They put too many rules in the way of worship.

Guru Nanak went to live and work in Sultanpur. He married and had two sons.

Every day Guru Nanak got up before dawn to bathe in the river. He would then **meditate** and pray (**B**). One morning Guru Nanak went to bathe and did not return. His friends found his clothes but no body.

In the presence of God

Three days later Guru Nanak appeared. He said he had been in the presence of

God. He had learnt the truth. Guru Nanak said there was no such thing as a Muslim or a Hindu. There was only one God and everyone was equal in the sight of God.

Discussion question

Do you agree with the view that people of different religions all worship the same God?

A Community

Guru Nanak spent the next 22 years of his life taking God's truth to the people. He travelled with two friends. Mardana the musician was a Muslim and Bala was a Hindu (**C**). After his travels Guru Nanak settled in the Punjab. He set up a community at Kartarpur. It was based on love for God and equality for all people.

C Guru Nanak with his friends Mardana and Bala

THINGS TO DO

1 Draw a time line to show the stages in the life of Guru Nanak.

2 What did Guru Nanak believe about:
   a God
   b human beings
   c religions?

3 Draw a map of India showing the Punjab. Write a sentence underneath to say why this is an important place for Sikhs.

4 Guru Nanak was sad about the divisions between people of different religions in his society. What are the divisions in our society today that would make Guru Nanak sad if he were alive now?

New words

Sikhs   Guru Nanak   meditate

The Ten Gurus

39

Choosing the next Guru

As Guru Nanak grew old he knew he had to choose someone to carry on his work after him. He had two sons. One was a holy man who lived alone in the forest, **fasting** and meditating. The other was a businessman, interested in making money.

Guru Nanak said that the true Sikh should live and work in the world and still love and serve God. So neither of the two sons was a good example of a true Sikh.

Angad

Guru Nanak thought about many of his followers. In the end he chose Lehna. He gave him the name **Angad**. Angad means 'limb from my own body'. Guru Nanak trusted Angad to carry on his work.

The death of Guru Nanak

When Guru Nanak died there was concern about what to do with the body. The Muslims wanted to bury the body according to their way. The Hindus wanted to **cremate** the body according to their beliefs.

In the end it was decided that both parties should leave flowers by the body of Guru Nanak. Those whose flowers were still fresh the next day would be able to decide the funeral (**A**).

Discussion question

What do you think Guru Nanak would have had to say about this disagreement over his funeral?

The next morning the flowers on both sides were fresh. But there was no body, only the white cloth that covered it. The two groups divided the cloth. The Muslims buried their half and the Hindus cremated theirs.

A What is the meaning of the story of the death of Guru Nanak?

There were nine **successors** to Guru Nanak. Together with him they are called **The Ten Gurus** (**B**). The word Guru means spiritual teacher. The Ten Gurus laid the foundations of the faith.

Guru Nanak 1469–1539
Guru Angad 1504–52
Guru Amardas 1479–1574
Guru Ram Das 1534–81
Guru Arjan 1563–1606
Guru Har Gobind 1595–1644
Guru Har Rai 1630–61
Guru Har Krishan 1656–64
Guru Tegh Bahadur 1621–75
Guru Gobind Singh 1666–1708

B The Ten Gurus of Sikhism

THINGS TO DO

1 What should a true Sikh do according to Guru Nanak? Write an advert or design a symbol to represent the true Sikh.

2 Is it hard to be religious in the world today? Write down three reasons to say why this might be true.

3 Tell the story of the body of Guru Nanak in words and pictures (**A**).

4 Look at the poster of the Ten Gurus (**B**). Which ten good people would you choose to put on a poster? Choose people who have made the world a better place.

New words

fasting   Angad   cremate
successors   The Ten Gurus

40

Symbols and beliefs

Sikhs believe in One God. There are many names to describe God. One name Sikhs use is **Sat Nam**. This means the True Name. Another is **Waheguru**. This is translated as Wonderful Lord.

The Mool Mantar

Sikhs do not represent God in pictures. They describe him in the words of the **Mool Mantar**:

> There is one and only One God
> Truth is His name
> He is the Creator
> He is without fear
> He is without hate
> Immortal
> He is beyond birth and death
> He is self-illuminated
> He is realized by the Grace of the
>   True Guru.

A The Mool Mantar in Punjabi, showing the Ik Onkar

The symbol **Ik Onkar** (**A**) is used to represent one God. But there are no images or pictures of God in the **gurdwara** which is the Sikh place of worship (**B**).

B There are no images of God in the Sikh place of worship, the gurdwara

C The symbol of the khanda

The symbol of the khanda

Another important Sikh symbol is the
khanda (**C**). The sword in the centre
symbolizes the One Supreme Truth.
The circle shows that God is without
beginning and without end. The two
swords stand for two kinds of strength.
One represents spiritual strength.
The other represents the strength to act.
Sikhs must pray and meditate. They must
also be ready to work hard and protect
the weak.

Beliefs in God as creator

Sikhs believe that God created the
universe. He created every living creature
and every human being. Everyone is a
member of God's family. Everyone is equal
in God's sight.

Discussion question

Why do people want to know how the
universe began and how human life began?

Sikhs believe in reincarnation. They say
that when a person dies the soul survives.
It is born into a new body and begins a
new life on earth. Sikhs believe we have
lived many lives in the past including
animal lives. Being born as a human is an
important step in coming close to God.
To become close to God, people need to
give up thoughts about themselves and
turn their thoughts and minds to God.

New words

Sat Nam	Mool Mantar	
Ik Onkar	gurdwara	khanda

THINGS TO DO

1 Design a car sticker for Sikhs using the
Sikh symbols. Explain the meaning of
the symbols.

2 Is it hard to have a balance between
quiet and busy time? Write a letter to a
newspaper which explains why schools
should help young people to find times
to be quiet as well as times to be busy
at work.

3 Draw two kinds of people, one who is
full of thoughts about themselves and
one who is learning to come close to
God. Write a sentence under each to say
what the differences are.

4 Write down your beliefs about:
   a the existence of God
   b how the universe came to be
   c what happens after death.
   Now write what a Sikh would say about
   each of these.

41 Symbols in Sikh worship

There are many ways to show that something is special. For example, a crown can show that a person is important.

Sikhs show that their holy scriptures are special and important by the signs and symbols they use.

Discussion question

What other examples of symbols can you think of to show that something or someone is special?

Guru Gobind Singh

The Tenth Guru, **Guru Gobind Singh**, said there would be no living Guru after him. The holy scriptures would be like a Guru to guide the community. The Sikh scriptures are called the **Guru Granth Sahib**. It contains the teachings of the Sikh Gurus and other religious teachers.

Showing respect

The Guru Granth Sahib is treated with great respect as if it were a living Guru (**A**). It is placed on a platform called a **takht**. There is usually a canopy over it. Beautiful cloths are used to wrap the scriptures. When the book is open a fan called a chauri is waved over the pages. This was once a way of showing respect to important people.

A The Guru Granth Sahib is treated with great respect

B Eating together and sharing food is a powerful symbol of equality

When the Guru Granth Sahib is not being used, it rests on a bed in a special room. It is covered in beautiful silk cloths. These are given by worshippers and they are called **rumalas**.

Blessed food

During the service at the gurdwara special food is offered to the worshippers. It is called **karah parshad**. This means blessed food. It is a symbol of God's grace and goodness. Every gurdwara has a **langar** or kitchen. This is where food is prepared for the community meal after the service (**B**). Eating together is an important symbol showing that everyone is equal.

New words

Guru Gobind Singh
Guru Granth   Sahib   takht
rumalas   karah   parshad   langar

THINGS TO DO

1 Draw the Guru Granth Sahib in the gurdwara. Show the platform, the canopy and the chauri and say what these represent.

2 What objects do you keep in a special place? Write down three things that are special to you and say how you keep them safe.

3 What signs or symbols would you use to show that everyone is equal in your school?

4 If you were to make a collection of writings that are important to you what would they be? Write a list of six books or texts that you would include.

The Five Ks

The **Five Ks** are important symbols worn by Sikhs who are members of the **Khalsa**. The Khalsa is made up of Sikhs who closely follow the Guru's teachings.

Kesh

Kesh (A) is clean, uncut hair. It is a symbol of commitment and a reminder of the purity and good order needed in a Sikh's life.

Guru Nanak introduced the turban as a way of keeping hair tidy. However, it is not one of the Five Ks. Sikhs believe that hair is a gift from God and should not be cut.

Kangha

The **kangha (B)** is the small wooden comb. This holds the hair in place. It is a symbol of cleanliness. As a comb removes tangles so the Sikh must get rid of selfish thoughts and actions in their life.

Discussion question

The way a person wears their hair is sometimes saying something important. What examples can you think of?

Kara

The **kara (B)** is the circular bracelet. It reminds a Sikh of their link with God. The circle, like God, has no beginning and no end.

A Kesh

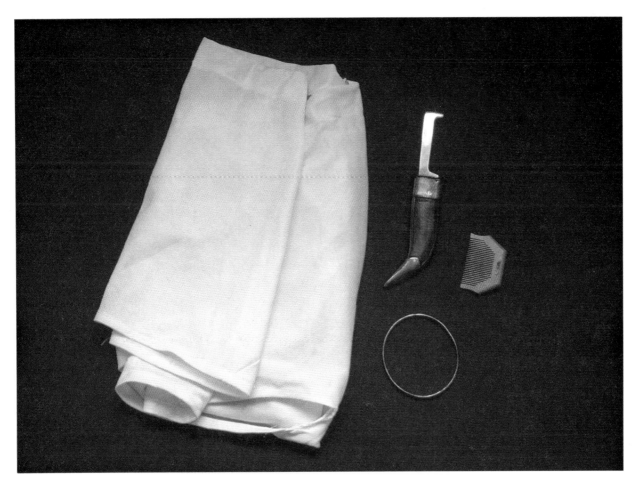

B Kangha, kara, kachera and kirpan

Kachera

Kachera (**B**) is the name for the shorts. These replaced the long cloth that used to be worn round the waist. Shorts make movement easier. This reminds Sikhs that they are meant to be active in doing good.

Kirpan

The **kirpan** (**B**) is the sword. Kirpa means an act of kindness. Aan means self-respect. The kirpan stands for self-respect and fearlessness in the face of evil and injustice.

New words

Five Ks   Khalsa   kesh   kangha
kara   kachera   kirpan

THINGS TO DO

1 If you asked a Sikh friend why they wear the Five Ks, what would they say? Write the answer.

2 Design a poster of the Five Ks. Label the symbols and explain what they mean.

3 What important qualities would you look for in a good person? Write down five qualities and explain why you chose them.

4 Design your own symbols for the qualities you have chosen in question 3.

43 Baisakhi

Special days

The special days during the Sikh year are called **gurpurbs**. The word means the Guru's remembrance day. Some gurpurbs mark the death of one of the Ten Gurus. Others celebrate the birthday of a Guru. For example, many Sikhs celebrate the birthday of Guru Nanak.

Akhand Path

At every gurpurb there is usually an **Akhand Path**. This is a non-stop reading of the Guru Granth Sahib from beginning to end. The gurdwara is open 24 hours a day. Worshippers come and listen and receive karah parshad.

The birth of the Khalsa

One of the best loved festivals is **Baisakhi**. This marks the birth of the Khalsa which is made up of committed Sikhs.

Guru Gobind Singh called all Sikhs together at the Indian festival of Baisakhi in 1699. At this time Sikhs were being attacked for their religion. Guru Gobind Singh said they would have to stand up for their religion. He asked for five volunteers who would be willing to give up their lives for their faith.

One by one five Sikhs came forward. Guru Gobind Singh took each one into his tent. Each time he came out with his sword dripping with blood.

Discussion question

Look at the pictures of Guru Nanak in Unit 38 and Guru Gobind Singh in this unit. How can you tell that they are serving their people in different ways?

The five Pure Ones

Eventually, Guru Gobind Singh came out with all five Sikhs alive (**A**). He gave them amrit, which is water sweetened with sugar. These Sikhs became known as the **Panj Piare**, the Pure Ones. They were the first members of the Sikh Khalsa. They had to follow a code of behaviour:

- to follow the teachings of the Gurus
- to offer daily prayers
- to give to charity
- to avoid tobacco and alcohol
- to be faithful in marriage
- to avoid the rituals of other relig'
- to wear the five Ks.

A Guru Gobind Singh with the Panj Piare

B Baisakhi celebrations in the UK

At Baisakhi Sikhs remember the faith of the Panj Piare. They go to the gurdwara to listen to the Guru Granth Sahib and share food in the langar. Some Sikh communities have processions in the street (**B**).

New words

gurpurbs   Akhand Path   Baisakhi
Panj Piare

THINGS TO DO

1 Tell the story of Baisakhi as a comic strip. Use words and pictures.

2 Answer the following questions in full sentences:
  a What is a gurpurb?
  b What is an Akhand Path?
  c Which Guru is remembered at Baisakhi?
  d Who are the Panj Piare?
  e What happens at Baisakhi?

3 Design an invitation to the celebration of Baisakhi at the gurdwara.

4 Describe a time when you have had to stand up for what you believe.

44 Amritsar

Guru Ram Das

Guru Ram Das was the fourth Guru. He was a good and humble Sikh. Men and women came to listen to him teach.

Guru Ram Das saw the need for a Sikh centre and city. He bought a piece of land in the Punjab (see the map on page 78). Here he set up a Sikh community. Two great pools were dug and small huts were built to house visitors. A free langar was set up to feed people coming to see the Guru. In time a small town grew up. This was known as Chak Guru Ram Das.

Guru Ram Das wanted the town to flourish. He invited craftsmen to come and settle. The town grew into a city. It became known as **Amritsar**. This means pool of nectar.

The Golden Temple

Today the city is a centre of trade and learning. There are many famous buildings. The best known is the **Golden Temple** (**A**). It was built by **Guru Arjun**. Sikhs call it the **Darbar Sahib**. It stands on an island in the centre of a pool. It has four entrances. This is to show that people from every corner of the world are welcome. In the centre of the Darbar Sahib is a special room where the Guru Granth Sahib is read throughout the day (**B**).

Discussion question

Do you think that a religion should open its doors to all people no matter what their beliefs?

A The Golden Temple at Amritsar

Guru Nanak taught his followers that people do not need to visit holy places to feel close to God. He said that Sikhs could find God in their everyday lives. But many Sikhs do like to go to Amritsar to see the Darbar Sahib. They go to remember the teachings of the Gurus. Some bathe in the sacred pool. Others visit the museums and buildings.

A special place

Amritsar is a special place for all Sikhs. The Punjab is where Sikhism began. Today the area of the Punjab is split by the border between India and Pakistan. Many Sikhs would like the Punjab to be one united country, not split in two.

New words

Guru Ram Das   Amritsar
Golden Temple
Guru Arjun   Darbar Sahib

B The Guru Granth Sahib is read in the Golden Temple throughout the day

THINGS TO DO

1 In words and pictures show three stages in the growth of the holy city of Amritsar.

2 Write down three reasons why Sikhs like to visit the Punjab and Amritsar.

3 If you wanted to set up a perfect community where people lived and worked peacefully together, what would be your rules for living? Write down six.

4 Design a poster made up of words, symbols and pictures inviting Sikhs to visit Amritsar.

Religion and meaning

Six religions

The six religions introduced in this book have different beliefs and different ways of doing things. But some of the things they are saying are the same.

All the religions say that there is a way to live that is not based on greed. They offer a way that is not based on having the most money, or the newest car, or the greatest political power.

All the religions say that we should think about the good of others and take responsibility for what we do. They all teach truth, love, peace and kindness to others.

Discussion question

Do you think that people from the different religions can learn from one another?

The blind men and the elephant

Some people argue that there is not just one religion that has all the truth. It is a bit like the story of the blind men and the elephant. A blind man and his blind friends were wanting to find out what an elephant was like. They began to touch the animal. One man said it was like a pillar. He had found the animal's leg. The second said it was like a fan. He had hold of the elephant's ear. The third said it was like a rope. He was holding the tail. The fourth and fifth all had their own ideas having found the belly and the trunk. No one had gathered the whole truth about the animal.

A Hindus celebrating God as Mother in the festival of Durga Puja

B The symbols of bread and light are important in Christianity

Religion and conflict

People of different religions often have very different beliefs about what the truth is. This is why there has been so much conflict over religion. Religion has sometimes brought out the bad side of people. But it has also brought out the good side in people. For many believers their religion has helped them to find a way to live and a way to love others. By looking at the different religions we can find out how people respond to the deeper questions of life. We are then in a better position to explore and express our own beliefs.

THINGS TO DO

1 Draw a chart to show six religions. Fill in examples to show one symbol, one festival, one special person and one special place for each religion.

2 Tell your own version of the story of the blind men. Say what you think it means.

3 Look at the photos in this unit. Write a sentence about what you think is happening in each photo.

4 Work in a group to prepare a presentation on one religion. Say what you have learnt about the religion and why you chose it.

C Sikh procession for Guru Nanak's birthday

Glossary

A

Abraham first well-known Jewish person. Muslims also believe he was a prophet called Ibrahim

Advent the time of preparation before Christmas

Akhand Path a complete reading of Sikh scriptures from beginning to end without a break

Allah Islamic name for God

Amritsar city in the Punjab where the Golden Temple is – a holy place for Sikhs

Angad name given to Guru Nanak's successor meaning a limb e.g. arm or leg

Anointed marked with oil. This is often part of a ceremony to make someone a king

Apostles followers of Jesus Christ

Ark a boat built by Nuh in the story of the flood

Arti a Hindu ceremony to welcome God at which light is offered

Aum a Hindu sacred sound and symbol

B

Baisakhi Sikh festival to celebrate the birth of the Khalsa

Baptized to have taken part in baptism a ceremony which welcomes a person into the Christian faith using water

Bhikkus Buddhist monks

Bhikkunis Buddhist nuns

Blessing gift showing God's love and goodness

Bodhi tree Gotama Buddha meditated under one of these and achieved enlightenment

Bodhisattva someone who puts off becoming a Buddha in order to help others

Bodhisattva Avalokiteshvara a spiritual being who helps others out of compassion

Brahma Hindu god of creation. One of the three faces of God

Brahman Hindu supreme spirit, universal spirit, God

Buddha Enlightened Being; someone who understands the truth about life

Buddhists people who follow the teachings of Gotama Buddha

C

Canaan the home of the Children of Israel. It is now called Israel

Covenant an agreement

Christmas festival when Christians remember the birth of Jesus Christ

Cremate to burn a dead body to ashes

Cross symbol of Christianity. It reminds Christians of the death and resurrection of Jesus Christ

Crucified crucifixion was a method of execution used by the Romans. Criminals were fastened to crosses and left to die

Crucifix Christian symbol of Jesus Christ on the cross

D

Darbar Sahib The Golden Temple in the Sikh holy city of Amritsar

Denominations different branches of the Christian Church

Dhamma the teachings of the Buddha

Dharma duty, law, religious duty for Hindus

Disciples followers or learners

Durga one name for the Hindu mother goddess

E

Easter Christian celebration of the resurrection of Jesus Christ

Eightfold Path Gotama Buddha's guidelines for living

Elijah a prophet. Jews believe he will come back to the world

Enlightenment understanding the truth about life

Esala Perahera the Buddha's tooth relic festival in Kandy

F

Fast to go without food or drink for religious reasons or beliefs

Five Ks five sacred symbols worn by those who have promised to be true Sikhs

G

Ganesha elephant-headed Hindu God. Symbol of the power to overcome things that get in the way of worship

Gentile someone who is not a Jew

Goddess female god

Golden Temple Sikh temple and place of pilgrimage at Amritsar

Gospels the books in the Christian Bible which tell about the life of Jesus Christ

Gurdwara Sikh place of worship

Gurpurb special day to celebrate or remember the life of one of the Sikh Gurus

Guru spiritual teacher, religious teacher

Guru Arjun fifth Sikh Guru

Guru Gobind Singh tenth Sikh Guru

Guru Granth Sahib Sikh holy scriptures

Guru Nanak first Sikh Guru and founder of the Sikh religion

Guru Ram Das fourth Sikh Guru

H

Hagadah a book used during the Jewish festival of Pesach

Haj Muslim pilgrimage to Makkah

Hanukkah 'dedication'. A Jewish winter festival which lasts for eight days

Hindu someone who believes in the Hindu religion

Holocaust the suffering and death of six million Jews in the Second World War

Holy Spirit part of the Christian Trinity of God. God's presence in the world

I

Ibrahim for Muslims, a prophet of Allah. Christians and Jews call him Abraham

Icons paintings used to help worship in Christian Orthodox churches

Idol statue or picture, which is worshipped in the place of God

Id-ul-Adha Muslim festival of sacrifice

Id-ul-Fitr Muslim festival of fast breaking at the end of Ramadan

Ihram white clothing worn by Muslims at Hajj as a sign of equality

Ik Onkar Sikh symbol meaning there is only One God

Incense substance burnt for its sweet smell used by Hindus as an offering to God

Interpret to work out the meaning

Islam faith followed by Muslims. It means submission or giving in, peace

Israel another name for the Jewish community. The country of Israel

J

Janmashtami Hindu festival celebrating birth of Krishna

Jerusalem holy city in Israel

Jesus Christ called The Son of God by Christians. With the Father and the Holy Spirit makes up the Trinity of God

Jews people belonging to the faith of Judaism or those born to Jewish mothers

K

Ka'bah Muslim sacred house of Allah at Makkah built by the prophet Ibrahim

Kachera shorts worn by Sikhs as underwear, one of the Five Ks

Kali one of the names of the Hindu mother goddess

Kali yuga age of darkness. The last of the four ages in the Hindu cycle

Kangha comb worn in the hair, one of the Five Ks

Kara steel bracelet, one of the Five Ks

Karah parshad blessed food shared at Sikh worship

Karma in Hinduism action, the effects or results of action on the person who acts

Kathina robe-giving ceremony for Buddhist monks and nuns

Kesh uncut hair, one of the Five Ks

Khalsa the community of those who have promised to be true Sikhs

Khanda double-edged sword used as a symbol in the Sikh flag and emblem

Kirpan sword worn by members of Khalsa, one of the Five Ks

Kosher 'fit'. Foods which Jews are allowed to eat

Krishna much-loved Hindu god, the human form taken by Vishnu when he came to earth

L

Langar Sikh kitchen where food is prepared and shared at the gurdwara. Also the name for the shared meal

Lay ordinary men and women of a religious community who are not priests or monks or nuns

Lent the time leading up to the festival of Easter

M

Magi men who came from the east to visit Jesus Christ soon after he was born

Mahayana one of the main types of Buddhism

Makkah Muslim holy city and centre of pilgrimage, birthplace of Muhammad

Mary the mother of Jesus Christ

Meditation being still, thinking about God in quiet thought and prayer

Merit in Buddhism spiritual reward for good works

Mezuzah a scroll with words from the Torah written on it. It is put on doorposts of Jewish

homes and is often in a small container

Mihrab small arch in Muslim mosque wall showing direction of Makkah

Miracle a wonderful event which cannot be explained

Missionaries people who spread religious teachings

Mool Mantar Sikh prayer or statement about God summed up in words of Guru Nanak

Monastery where monks live

Monks men who give up ordinary life to live a strict religious life

Moses the man who led the Hebrew slaves out of Egypt. God gave him the Torah

Mosque Muslim place of prayer and worship

Muddas hand positions of Buddha rupas

Muhammad name of last of the prophets according to Muslim fatith

Murti an image of a Hindu god or goddess

Muslim a follower of the faith of Islam one who gives in to the will of Allah

N

New Testament the second part of the Christian Bible

Nibbana a state of perfect peace

Nuh one of the prophets of Allah in the Muslim Qur'an also in the Jewish and Christian scriptures – known as Noah

O

Orthodox Churches branches of the Christian Church

P

Pali Canon Buddhist scriptures written in the Pali language

Panj Piare the Five Pure Ones, the first members of the Sikh Khalsa chosen by Guru Gobind Singh

Pesach Jewish spring festival which celebrates the escape of the Hebrew slaves from Egypt

Pilgrimage a journey with a religious purpose or meaning

Pope head of the Roman Catholic Church

Prophet someone sent by God to speak God's message

Puja Hindu word for worship, usually at a shrine

Purim a Jewish festival

Q

Qur'an the Muslim sacred scriptures

R

Rains retreat a time when Buddhist monks and nuns stay in their monasteries instead of travelling to teach others

Rama Hindu god, Vishnu came to earth to save

Ramadan a month of fasting in the Muslim calendar

Relic part of the remains of a person which is used as a memorial

Resurrection the rising from death of Jesus Christ

Revelation something that is revealed or made clear, shown by God to humankind

Ritual religious action, something someone does that has religious meaning

Roman Catholic a branch of the Christian Church

Rosh Hashanah Jewish New Year

Rumala silk cloth to wrap the Sikh scriptures

Rupas images of the Buddha

S

Sacrifice an offering of something precious or valued

Salvation Army a branch of the Christian Church

Sangha sometimes means the community of Buddhist monks and nuns and sometimes means the whole Buddhist community

Sat Nam The True Name, Sikh title for God

Seder 'order'. It is the name given to the special meal eaten during the Jewish festival of Pesach

Shabbat weekly holy day for Jews

Shavuot a Jewish festival

Shayton Satan or the devil

Shema an important Jewish prayer

Shiva Hindu God, Lord of destruction, one of the three faces of God

Shofar ram's horn blown at Rosh Hashanah

Shrine a place or container with an image of a god or goddess used for worship

Sikh a follower of the Sikh faith meaning disciple or follower, someone who is seeking God

Society of Friends a branch of the Christian Church sometimes called the Quakers

Stations of the Cross pictures which tell the story of the end of Jesus Christ's life

Stupa Buddhist burial mound

Successor someone who continues the work of a leader

Sukkot a Jewish harvest festival. Jews build temporary booths to live in for this time

Synagogues Jewish place of meeting, prayer and study

T

Takht platform on which Guru Granth Sahib is raised in the gurdwara

Tallit a garment with four corners and fringes worn by many Jewish men sometimes when they pray

Tawaf the act of walking around the Ka'bah as part of the Muslim Hajj

Tawhid belief that God is One and there is no other like God

Tefillin small leather boxes. Inside are quotations from the Torah. They are strapped to the forehead and arm by some Jews for weekday morning prayers

Temple a place of worship

Ten Commandments or Ten Sayings. Ten rules found in the Torah

Ten Gurus the line of ten gurus who were the leaders and teachers of the Sikh faith

Theravada one of the main types of Buddhism

Three Jewels Buddha, Dhamma and Sangha

Torah law or teaching. The Five Books of Moses

Tzizit fringes for the tallit and the undervest worn by some Jewish men

U

Uposatha special days in the Buddhist calendar

V

Vajrayana one type of Buddhism

Varanasi also called Benares, Hindu place of pilgrimage on the banks of river Ganges in India

Vatican the centre of the Roman Catholic Church

Vedas the oldest most holy of the Hindu scriptures

Vishnu Hindu god, the Preserver, one of the three faces of God

W

Wesak a Buddhist festival when many Buddhists celebrate the birth, enlightenment and death of the Buddha

Wudu washing before Muslim worship as a sign of respect

Y

Yoga control of mind, body and way of life in order to come closer to God

Yom Kippur Jewish Day of Atonement following Rosh Hashanah

Z

Zakat-ul-Fitr money or other form of giving to those in need because God asks it